*How to Make
the Transition from
an Entrepreneurship
to a Professionally
Managed Firm*

Eric G. Flamholtz

How to Make
the Transition from
an Entrepreneurship
to a Professionally
Managed Firm

106504

Jossey-Bass Publishers

San Francisco • London • 1986

HOW TO MAKE THE TRANSITION FROM AN ENTREPRENEURSHIP TO A
PROFESSIONALLY MANAGED FIRM
by Eric G. Flamholtz

Copyright © 1986 by: Jossey-Bass Inc., Publishers
433 California Street
San Francisco, California 94104

&

Jossey-Bass Limited
28 Banner Street
London EC1Y 8QE

Library of Congress Cataloging-in-Publication Data

Flamholtz, Eric.
How to make the transition from an entrepreneurship to
a professionally managed firm.

(The Jossey-Bass management series)
Bibliography: p. 219
Includes index.
1. New business enterprises—Management.   2. Organi-
zational change.   I. Title.   II. Series.
HD62.5.F535   1986   658.4′063   85-45902
ISBN 0-87589-679-0

Manufactured in the United States of America

The paper in this book meets the guidelines for
permanence and durability of the Committee on
Production Guidelines for Book Longevity of the
Council on Library Resources.

JACKET DESIGN BY WILLI BAUM

FIRST EDITION

Code 8610

The Jossey-Bass
Management Series

To my daughter, Laurie

Preface

Entrepreneurship has increased throughout the economy during the past few years, and there have been a large number of remarkable entrepreneurial successes. Companies in businesses as diverse as pizza, computers, women's fashion, chocolate chip cookies, bioengineering, printing, publishing, distribution, and real estate, to cite just a few, have flourished. Some entrepreneurships have become spectacular successes and household names, including Apple Computer Inc., Liz Claiborne, Mrs. Fields' Cookies, Federal Express, and Domino's Pizza. Many more relatively unknown firms have also been considerably successful.

There have also been a significant number of entrepreneurial failures. Some firms, after a brilliant start, merely lose their luster. Others that exhibit initial meteoric success experience equally meteoric failure. Some entrepreneurial failures, such as Osborne Computer Corporation, are well publicized, but the majority are more private disappointments.

In addition to the success or failure of the overall enterprise, there has been a high degree of turnover among the founders of entrepreneurial companies. Some of the most well known cases of entrepreneurial founders who were later replaced include Steven Jobs and Jack Tramiel. Steven Jobs of Apple Computer gave way to John Sculley, who was brought in from Pepsico to help professionalize the company. Jack Tramiel resigned from Commodore International, apparently responding to similar circumstances. A company spokesman said that Tramiel and other people in the organization wanted the company to have more discipline and structure, and that Tramiel felt this could only happen if he stepped down.

There is a pattern to what happened at Apple, Commodore, Osborne, and many other entrepreneurial companies. In brief, all of these firms and their founders faced the need to make a transition from an entrepreneurship to a professionally managed organization. Unfortunately, while all of their founders had the skills and personality to establish a successful entrepreneurship, not all of them possessed the very different skills, behavioral patterns, and will necessary to take the firm to the next stage of development. Adam Osborne, one of the most famous of entrepreneurs who experienced this phenomenon, seemed to understand it in retrospect. In reflecting on what had happened to Osborne Computer Corporation, Osborne said the firm "had existed only eighteen months in terms of operation—hardly time to get my feet wet; all of a sudden the job was a whole different order of magnitude. I realized it was no longer an entrepreneurial operation in any conceivable way."* The company had needed to change from what it had been during its initial period of rapid growth and success. Yet, the required transition had not been made and, consequently, the company ultimately failed.

This book is addressed to the owners, managers, and employees of entrepreneurial companies, to investors, bankers, and venture capitalists as well as to students and scholars of management, who are interested in the success and failure of entrepreneurships. It focuses on the question of why, after successful or even brilliant beginnings, entrepreneurial companies often lose their way and their luster. More important, it explains what entrepreneurial companies must do to be successful as they grow and describes the transitions they must make in order to survive. Case studies of entrepreneurial companies at different stages of growth are included to illustrate different aspects of the transitions that must be made

* Mamis, R. A. " 'Face to Face' with Adam Osborne." *Inc.*, November 1983, p. 22.

as well as how the framework provided in this book can be used as
a conceptual map of what needs to be done by an organization at
each developmental stage. The book also specifies the adjustments
the founder or chief executive officer of an entrepreneurial company
needs to make so that he or she can grow with the organization and
not be left behind, as Steven Jobs and Adam Osborne were.

The basic theme of the book, as indicated by its title, is how
to make the successful transition from an entrepreneurship to a
professionally managed organization. Some people may conclude
that because I suggest that entrepreneurships must make transitions
and become something else I am negative about entrepreneurships,
but this is hardly the case. I admire the entrepreneur, not only as an
individual willing to bet his or her future on an idea but also as the
critical element of our economy and the vanguard of the future. But
I believe that at some stage entrepreneurship is not sufficient and
that the nature of the organization must change, together with the
people who run it.

For some people the phrase "professional management" has
negative connotations. They see it as synonymous with "bureaucracy." In my view, however, a professionally managed firm has
achieved the best of both worlds. It is entrepreneurial without
entrepreneurship being its only strength; it is well managed
without becoming choked on its own systems and procedures. An
analogy might be a great sports team that has an excellent offense
as well as a superb defense. Entrepreneurship is the essence of an
organization's offense, while effective management is the essence of
its defense. Just as a great defense can create opportunities for the
offense, so can the management systems initiated by professional
managers create opportunities for entrepreneurship.

This book is the outgrowth of more than ten years of research
and consulting experience with many entrepreneurships as well as
with large institutional organizations. My interest in this area
began in 1976 when I was asked to assist the president of a small
entrepreneurial firm in the health care industry in learning how to
manage his business. This individual was a medical doctor who had
started a business but knew relatively little about managing an
organization. Since he was the president of a rapidly growing
company, he did not have time to take two years off to get an MBA.

Nor was he interested in the MBA "label"; he just wanted the knowledge base. Accordingly, I was asked to work with him as a tutor and provide him with a personalized on-the-job MBA-type education. The challenge to me was to draw on the concepts and methods I had been teaching to students at universities such as Columbia, Michigan, and the University of California at Los Angeles (UCLA) and tailoring the material for an entrepreneur who was actually facing the day-to-day risks and pressures of building and running a business. I had to sift through such esoteric concepts as capital budgeting, responsibility accounting, MBO, Markov chains, Theory X and Y, socio-technical systems, and myriad others to determine which were really useful in managing a business. It was a fascinating experience.

Within a few years other people had learned about the work I was doing with entrepreneurial organizations and I found myself working with a number of companies of differing sizes in such varied industries as executive search, electronics manufacturing, residential real estate, industrial abrasives distribution, commercial banking, public accounting, garment manufacturing, advertising, mortgage banking, publishing, furniture manufacturing, public accounting, financial planning, motorcycle manufacturing, printing, law firms, restaurant management, and electronic components distribution. In almost every case, the president of the company would say to me something like, "Our problems in my industry are unique." Initially I believed this myth, but I was trained as a researcher and I soon began to see common patterns in the problems and issues faced by this diverse set of companies, regardless of who the president was, irrespective of his or her personality or the nature of the industry.

Most, if not all, of the companies I was working to assist were successful firms. Their stories were quite similar: The entrepreneurs had been able to identify markets and develop suitable products or services that were geared to their markets' needs. Then they began to experience rapid growth. At some point in the growth process, a variety of problems surfaced in each organization: people were working harder and harder but were still unable to keep up with the load; people were spending too much time going from crisis to crisis; no one ever had time to do anything "right" the first time;

there was too much duplication of effort; the entrepreneur was becoming a bottleneck; lots of people had the title of "manager" but there were relatively few good managers in the company; the organization's meetings were frustrating and were perceived as a waste of time; people had begun to grumble about their company's lack of direction; some people began to feel insecure about their places in the company and were spending an increasing percentage of their time covering their "vested interests." In brief, I perceived that regardless of the differences in personalities and industries, each of these companies as well as their founders and managers were facing a common overarching problem: the need to make a transition from an entrepreneurship to a professionally managed organization. This transition required stepping back from the day-to-day activities of the enterprise and understanding that the company's very success had created the need for a different kind of organization and a different style of management. The new challenge to senior management was to rethink the kind of organization that was needed in the new firm that the enterprise had become. Most of these entrepreneurs were having difficulty managing their organizations' growth because they did not have a "game plan" for developing their enterprises; rather, they were too preoccupied with day-to-day issues.

My academic training had taught me to study the published literature for research that might provide insights into the problems these companies faced. Unfortunately, I found that most of the literature addressed the functions of management, such as planning, organizing, and controlling, and the tools of business administration, such as statistics, accounting, and economics. The issues involved in organizational transitions were virtually ignored.

I may have been especially sensitive to those transition issues because I was on the faculty at UCLA and am an ardent basketball fan. I was well aware that John Wooden, who is widely regarded as the greatest coach in the history of basketball, was a master of the "transition game"—the change from offense to defense and back again. I also understood that Wooden was, in essence, a manager who had built a basketball dynasty because he was able to think conceptually about the game as well as operationally. That is, he could not only see his team and its competition as strategically evolving wholes but could also focus on the day-to-day "nuts and bolts" aspects of coaching.

With these many ideas on the topic fusing and forming in my mind, I began to do research on how and why some firms are successful in managing the stages of entrepreneurial growth while others are not. I also wanted to see if it were feasible to develop a method or approach that organizations could use to successfully make the transition from one stage to the next. I used the real world of organizations as my laboratory, analyzing the data I had obtained from actual companies I had worked with as a consultant. I was fortunate in having the opportunity to work as a consultant, researcher, and management development specialist with a number of large, successful, professionally managed firms which are among Fortune's 500. These include some of the most successful U.S. companies and range from such industrial enterprises as aerospace, business equipment manufacturing, petroleum refining and distribution, public utilities, and consumer goods manufacturing, as well as other high- and low-tech manufacturing businesses, to such service industries as public accounting, banking, insurance, residential and commercial real estate, and hotel management. From this experience, I was able to formulate ideas about what made companies successful. Out of this research evolved my theory of the pyramid of organizational development, described in Chapter One, which explains the key factors in developing a successful and profitable organization. I also developed a framework that identifies seven different stages of organizational growth, and the key organizational development issues at each stage. Moreover, from an analysis of the problems experienced by rapidly growing entrepreneurial organizations I identified a set of ten classic growing pains and developed a method of measuring these symptoms of organizational difficulty (described in Chapter Three). Using the Organizational Growing Pains Questionnaire, I began to collect a data base on organizational growing pains experienced by organizations in different industries and at different stages of growth. My associates and I have used this data base to conduct a variety of research studies, some of which are included in this book. Taken together, this research led to the ideas presented in Part One, "A Framework for Developing Successful Organizations."

Moreover, I was able to put this theory into practice with a number of companies that were faced with the need to move from one stage of growth to the next. This "action research" was the basis of my ideas about how to successfully make the transition from an entrepreneurship to a professionally managed organization. It is described in the case studies that appear in Part Two, "Management Strategies for Each Stage of Organizational Growth."

My experience leads me to conclude that one of the key ingredients in successful organizational development is the entrepreneur's ability to think conceptually and strategically about the company, rather than merely in terms of products, people, and day-to-day operations. Some parts of this book require such conceptual and strategic thinking; that is, they require that we step back and view the organization in somewhat abstract terms. Entrepreneurs and their associates who master the framework provided here will be able to use it to understand where their organizations are in terms of current development and what their companies must do to continue to operate successfully.

Overview of the Contents

This book is divided into four related parts. Part One presents a conceptual framework for managers of entrepreneurial organizations to use in understanding what is happening to their firms and what they must do to achieve the next stage successfully. The framework includes the six key factors for developing an effective profitable organization and descriptions of the successive stages of organizational growth at which transitions must be made. Part One also describes the organizational growing pains that are common in rapidly growing firms and presents a method for assessing the extent to which an organization suffers from them.

Part Two presents a series of organizational case studies as a vehicle for examining what an organization must do to develop successfully from one stage of organizational development to the next. Specifically, Part Two presents examples of companies at all the four critical stages of growth, from new venture to organizational maturity. It describes the problems those companies faced and explains how such problems need to be dealt with as an organization grows.

Part Three presents a primer of the most significant managerial tools that entrepreneurial organizations must master if they are to grow and develop successfully and profitably: strategic planning, organizational control, management development, and organizational leadership. Part Four deals with the transitions facing the presidents or chief executive officers of entrepreneurial organizations; it is designed to help them make their firms grow successfully—and grow personally along with them.

Entrepreneurship is a defining force in today's economy. Accordingly, it is important that entrepreneurial companies be successful, not only for the good of the entrepreneurs and their employees but also because of the benefits to the general economy of employment and technology that entrepreneurial organizations contribute. Unfortunately, too many entrepreneurial companies flounder after promising or even brilliant beginnings. Some cynical observers have even begun to define an entrepreneur as someone who can start and build a company to a given level and then watch it fail. My experience in doing research and consulting with entrepreneurial companies has led me to write this book to help present and potential entrepreneurs as well as their employees, advisors, and venture capitalists understand the pitfalls typically faced by entrepreneurial organizations at different stages of growth and to explain how to make the successful transition from entrepreneurship to professionally managed firm. Although this book will not solve all the problems faced by entrepreneurial companies, my experience indicates that if the ideas and methods described in this book are applied, organizations will have a significantly improved likelihood of continued success. My hope for this book is that it will prove of practical utility to one of our most valuable natural resources—the entrepreneur.

Acknowledgments

Although a book may bear the name of an individual as author, I doubt whether many manuscripts are ever completed without the assistance and significant contributions of a great many people. This is most certainly the case with the present volume, and I am indebted to several individuals for their support and assistance throughout the preparation of this book.

First, this work is a produc: of several years of consultation and action research with many different organizations. These companies ranged from new ventures to members of Fortune's 500. They were my research "laboratory." Simply stated, the most significant ideas that underlie this book were the products of observing, analyzing, and conceptualizing about what actually happened in successful and unsuccessful organizations as they grew. The book could not have been written without my having had access to those companies of differing sizes, in different industries, with differing degrees of success. Accordingly, I am greatly indebted to the CEOs, presidents, senior managers, and others who invited me to serve as researcher, consultant, or advisor for their organizations. (Most of these companies shall not be mentioned by name, to preserve their privacy. In some cases, fictitious names are used; in others, examples are cited without the company being named at all.) I am especially grateful to the two owners of the company disguised as "Tempo Products" in Chapter Six, who are referred to as "Ron" and "Cathy Forest Harrison," for their input concerning the chapter as well as their understanding of my desire to focus the chapter on those aspects of their company most relevant to this book.

Some other people also made significant contributions to the book. Special acknowledgment must be made to Yvonne Randle, Ph.D. candidate in the Graduate School of Management at the University of California, Los Angeles, who served as my research assistant at UCLA. She helped prepare the case studies presented in Chapters Five and Six and contributed to sections of the Introduction and Chapter Three. She also reviewed the entire manuscript and made suggestions for improvement. Her skill, motivation, enthusiasm, ability to work under stress, and good humor were invaluable and are gratefully acknowledged.

Chapter Nine, dealing with the role of management development in the transition from entrepreneurship to professional management, was coauthored by H. Stephen Cranston, president of Knapp Communications Corporation, who kindly read and made constructive comments on the entire manuscript. I am also indebted to C. T. "Bud" Knapp, chairman, and Elizabeth Wood Knapp, senior vice-president, of Knapp Communications Corporation for their invitation to work on the management development program described in Chapter Nine. They also took time from busy schedules to read and comment on the manuscript. Moreover, I want to express my appreciation and respect for their encouraging me to present my own views of what happened at Knapp Communications Corporation, even when our opinions differed.

I am indebted in several ways to the Graduate School of Management at the University of California at Los Angeles, for various kinds of support in connection with this book. First, I wish to acknowledge J. Clayburn La Force, dean of the Graduate School of Management, for his leadership in providing a supportive academic environment. The Price Institute for Entrepreneurial Studies, under the direction of Alfred Osborne, provided financial support for research assistance to prepare some of the case studies presented in this book. I have used the manuscript for this book as a text in a special topics course entitled Managing Entrepreneurial Organizations, which I developed in the Graduate School of Management at UCLA. I have also used portions of the manuscript in a series of seminars titled How to Make the Successful Transition from an Entrepreneurship to a Professionally Managed Firm, which I developed and have offered in cooperation with the Office of Executive Education, under the direction of Victor Tabush, at UCLA.

The word processing and preparation of the manuscript for this book were done by the operations support staff of Management Systems Consulting Corporation, especially by Karen Nitao under the direction of Robbie Amodio, operations coordinator. The data presented in Chapter Three is drawn from the organizational effectiveness data base compiled by Management Systems Consulting Corporation. It is derived from a questionnaire that I developed. I am also indebted to Russell Coff, research project coordinator, and Joanne Cotter, educational programs coordinator, both of Management Systems Consulting Corporation, who assisted in preparation and interpretation of the data dealing with

Preface**xix**

organizational growing pains (Chapter Three). Valerie Frank, a
consultant with Management Systems Consulting Corporation,
participated in some of the organizational studies cited in the book.
Sigal Goland and Joseph Van Winkle assisted with the preparation
of the annotated bibliography.

I am indebted to the staff of Jossey-Bass Publishers for the
highly professional and competent way in which this project was
handled. They were enthusiastic about this book from its inception
and supportive throughout its execution. Although company
policy prohibits mentioning individuals by name, I wish to
acknowledge my appreciation and respect for the people involved.
As with my previous book published by Jossey-Bass, it has been a
genuine pleasure to work with them.

Acknowledgment of a different kind is appropriate for Diana
Troik Flamholtz, my wife. As always, she provided personal and
professional support throughout the development of this book.

Although I acknowledge with gratitude the contributions of
all those cited above, I remain responsible for the book and its
imperfections.

*Los Angeles, California*Eric G. Flamholtz
February 1986

Contents

The Author

Eric G. Flamholtz is professor of management at the Graduate School of Management, University of California at Los Angeles, and assistant director of the Institute of Industrial Relations, University of California at Los Angeles, where he heads the Center for Research on Human Resource Management. His other administrative responsibilities have included vice-chairmanship of the Graduate School of Management and director of the Accounting-Information Systems Research Program. Flamholtz teaches courses in a variety of areas, including accounting-information systems, human resource management, planning and control systems, managerial decision making, and entrepreneurial management. He is also the president of Management Systems Consulting Corporation, which he founded in 1978.

Flamholtz received his Ph.D. degree from the University of Michigan, where he served on the staff of the Institute for Social Research under the direction of Rensis Likert. His doctoral dissertation, "The Theory and Measurement of an Individual's Value to an Organization," was cowinner of the McKinsey Foundation for Management Research Dissertation Award.

Flamholtz has also served on the faculties at Columbia University and the University of Michigan and has been a faculty fellow at Price Waterhouse & Co. He has broad interests in management and has done research on a variety of management topics, ranging from accounting and human resource management to organizational development and strategic planning. Flamholtz has conducted research projects for the National Science Foundation, the National Association of Accountants, and the U.S. Office of Naval Research.

The author of more than fifty articles and chapters on a variety of management topics, Flamholtz published *Human Resource Accounting* (2nd ed., Jossey-Bass) in 1985. Three other books are forthcoming: *Human Resource Management, Organizational Control,* and *Financial Accounting* (coauthored). He is in the process of completing an additional book titled *Principles of Accounting* (coauthored).

As a consultant, Flamholtz has extensive experience with firms ranging from entrepreneurships to members of the New York Stock Exchange and Fortune's 500. He has also presented seminars and management development programs for organizations in Belgium, France, West Germany, Greece, Mexico, and the People's Republic of China, as well as throughout the United States.

*How to Make
the Transition from
an Entrepreneurship
to a Professionally
Managed Firm*

Introduction: The Transitions Needed to Keep a Growing Firm Successful

Custom Printing Corporation: An Entrepreneurial Case Study

Joe McBride began working at Custom Printing Corporation while he was still in high school. He worked hard to learn all that he could about the printing business, since he had decided he wanted a career in this industry. Two years after Joe's graduation from high school, when the original owner of the print shop retired, Joe borrowed money from his parents and bought Custom Printing for $10,000. At that time, the shop employed two persons besides Joe.

As is true in most entrepreneurial firms, the early years of Joe's ownership involved great struggle. Custom Printing had a high sales volume but operated without a profit. However, after about seven years of simply staying afloat, the business began to grow. This growth resulted, in part, from Joe's ability to seek a new market niche for his company and to acquire the resources to create products and services that fitted this niche. Joe's strategy was to make Custom Printing a "service printer." This meant that it would serve a small number of customers who had high demands

1

for printing. This strategy proved successful, and in the decade between 1968 and 1978, the demand for Custom Printing's services grew so large that the company had to move to new facilities in order to accommodate it. In fact, during that decade, the company relocated its operations not once but twice.

After the final move in 1978, Joe decided to change his market niche by focusing a certain amount of effort on high-quality printing jobs such as limited edition prints and other artistic works. This helped Joe's customers begin to recognize that Custom Printing was more than just a "stationery printer." In 1980, the company's services expanded to include the production of annual reports for design companies. During this year, sales reached $10 million.

The Onset of "Growing Pains"

It was at about this time, in the early 1980s, that Custom Printing began to experience the typical symptoms of organizational growing pains. Some of these symptoms were more severe than others, but nearly all warranted attention. These symptoms will be discussed in order of severity, ranging from most to least severe.

People did not understand what their jobs were, what others' jobs were, or what the relationships were between their jobs and the jobs of others. This problem resulted, in part, from the company's tendency to add people without developing clear definitions of their roles and responsibilities. Custom Printing did not have a formal organization chart that clearly outlined roles, responsibilities, and relationships between positions and functions within the company.

Because of the lack of clearly defined roles and responsibilities, people did not know to whom they should report nor for what they could be held accountable. For example, no one seemed to know who was responsible for shipping and receiving, which led to a situation in which packages often got "lost in the system." Furthermore, no one seemed to want to be held responsible for this and other activities. As a result, departments and individuals were constantly bickering over who should be held accountable when mistakes (such as lost packages) occurred.

Other problems that resulted from the lack of clearly defined roles and responsibilities were duplication of effort and loss of productivity. People and departments came to feel that "I need to do the job myself if I want it to get done," which often resulted in more than one person performing the same task. At the same time, individuals often assumed that "someone else will do it," so some tasks never got done at all. The overlap between the sales and production departments was particularly noticeable.

The lack of clearly defined linkages between organizational roles meant unnecessary isolation as well as unnecessary overlap. The production department, for example, often ignored the cost that the estimating department had suggested for a job and, instead, did it "their way." This sometimes resulted in unanticipated changes in costs, which were not communicated to the estimating department because there was no standard procedure for doing so. Even within departments, there was a lack of needed communication. For example, production coordinators, who were responsible for integrating the various stages of jobs, often were not notified about production problems until days after they occurred because other employees did not understand the coordinators' function. These organizational deficiencies resulted in unnecessary delays in completing jobs and led to customer frustration.

The company had a sales orientation rather than a profit orientation. Custom Printing, like many entrepreneurial firms, traditionally had been most concerned with increasing its sales. It had operated under the premise that if sales were increased, profit would also be increased. This belief affected all areas of the company's operations. At the organizational level, management emphasized "keeping the presses running," since this symbolized the fact that the company was generating business. At times, however, this practice led to decreasing rather than increasing profits.

At the individual employee level, the notion that "profit would take care of itself if only sales were increased" was pervasive. The sales force held this belief very strongly. Salespeople believed that while the amount of sales was under their control, profit was not: as long as they were generating sales, profit would take care of itself.

As Custom Printing grew, its management began to realize that this sales orientation was adversely affecting the company. In order to continue to be successful, it needed to adopt a profit rather than a sales orientation. This became painfully evident when, in 1982, sales reached nearly $7 million, but the company had an operating loss of $120,000.

Employees in some departments felt "overloaded." In sales, the lack of comaraderie between employees was blamed on a lack of time during which important relationships between people could be developed. Salespeople felt pressure to generate and maintain customers, a job that at times seemed to require twenty-four hours a day. In production, controllers said that they often felt overloaded because they were forced to work long hours in order to complete the high number of rush orders on time.

Many employees at Custom Printing said they felt as if they were constantly trying to "catch up"; no matter how hard they worked, there always seemed to be more to do. Joe McBride, the company's owner, suffered from this feeling probably more than anyone, for he sometimes devoted up to sixteen hours a day to his business. This constant time pressure put most employees at Custom Printing under a great deal of stress. It was suggested that the high turnover the company experienced during the early 1980s was due to too much stress.

Employees spent a lot of time resolving short-term problems that resulted from the lack of long-range planning. The production department seemed to suffer most from this problem. Because of both a lack of communication between departments and a lack of planning, production was often forced to complete orders on a rush basis. More often than not, these jobs had to be redone because of mistakes. This resulted in unanticipated delays for customers and unanticipated costs for Custom Printing.

Poor communication between the production and shipping departments contributed to other problems in completing orders. For example, sometimes an order would be sent to shipping from production only to sit there for days either because shipping did not know what to do with it or because there was a backlog of other orders. When severe backlogs occurred, drivers had to be paid to work evenings and weekends, resulting in added costs for the company. At other times, when drivers weren't needed, they often simply sat around the plant, doing nothing.

Lack of planning also resulted in short-term crises for the purchasing and marketing departments. Purchasing did not acquire new vendors until there was a "falling out" with an existing one. This meant that the organization was sometimes disrupted by having to wait for needed supplies until a new vendor could be located. In the marketing department, problems with reports were dealt with only when they became severe enough to be brought to the marketing manager's attention.

There were not enough good managers. Some managers at Custom Printing were described as "managers in title only." These people did not perform effectively in managerial roles. Some people suggested that this ineffectiveness existed because the company gave the managers responsibility but no authority. Others suggested that certain managers simply did not possess the training or skills necessary to be effective. For example, the best salesman in the company had been promoted to a management position. Unfortunately, his ability to manage people was much lower than his ability to complete sales, and this was reflected in his areas' performance and his subordinates' morale.

Custom Printing did not have an overall business plan, and when plans were made, there was no follow-up. Custom Printing had traditionally operated on an *ad hoc* basis; long-range planning was never a concern. As the firm grew, however, management began to realize that it needed to make some sort of plan. Custom Printing was particularly concerned about setting and meeting financial goals related to sales and costs. Unfortunately, control systems to monitor performance on these and other goals had not been developed, so when goals were not met, there were no repercussions. Paperwork on sales, for example, was often not completed on time, yet no consistent action was taken to improve this situation.

Some employees felt that Custom Printing had no long-term goals. This was articulated in statements such as "Custom Printing lacks a presence" and "I don't know where the company is going." Such statements suggested that Custom Printing's management had failed to communicate its vision for the company to its employees. Employees were aware that changes were being made, but they did not know the ultimate goal toward which the changes were aimed. As a result, employees experienced a certain amount of anxiety and inability to focus their work.

Some people and departments felt they needed to do everything themselves. Because of the lack of clearly defined roles and responsibilities and of coordination between people and departments, each department worked independently of the others. If something needed to be done, people either did it themselves or placed the blame for not accomplishing it on another area or person.

Some people complained that meetings were a waste of time. This was particularly true in the sales area, where time spent in meetings was time taken away from customers. Salespeople had yet to realize the value of meetings in coordinating activities, even though they often complained about the lack of established territories and coordination of sales efforts.

Some people felt insecure in their place at the firm. This was another problem that grew out of the large number of changes in the company, combined with employees' lack of understanding of the company's long-range goals. The presence of high turnover suggested that some people may have left the firm because the anxiety of "living from day to day" and wondering what would happen next was too much to bear.

Recognizing the Need for a Transition

Joe McBride realized that despite his company's growth in sales, it was in trouble. He realized that he had to make changes in the way the company was operating as well as in his own style of running the business. He knew that both he and the firm had to make a transition from the present entrepreneurial style of operation to a more professional style of management.

Joe and his managers therefore began a four-step program to allow Custom Printing Corporation to make the transition from an entrepreneurship to a more professionally managed firm. The specific steps in the program were as follows:

Phase I: Assess the company's current state of development as an organization and its future development needs.

Phase II: Design a program for the development of the organization as a whole.

Phase III: Implement the organizational development program.

Phase IV: Monitor the program and make changes as needed.

Making the Transition: Phase I

In order to assess the company's current state of development and future needs, an organizational audit was performed. The audit involved collecting information from the company's employees about their perceptions of Custom Printing and its operations. One tool used in this process was the "Symptoms of Organizational Growing Pains Questionnaire" described in Chapter Three. The score that was calculated from responses to this questionnaire revealed the severity of the company's organizational growing pains and indicated that it was time for the company to make some changes. Specifically, the audit revealed that the company needed to

- define organizational roles and responsibilities and the linkages between roles;
- become profit oriented rather than strictly sales oriented;
- help employees plan and budget their time;
- develop a business plan and a system for monitoring it;
- increase the number of qualified present and potential managers;
- identify the direction the company should take in the future;
- reduce employee and departmental feelings that they always "need to do it themselves" if a job is to get done;
- reestablish the importance of meetings and make them more efficient.

Making the Transition: Phases II and III

Having identified its current needs, Custom Printing proceeded to the next step in its organizational development program: designing and implementing a program that would meet these needs and help the company prepare for its next stage of development. Management decided that the program should have three parts: (1) organization design, (2) strategic planning, and (3) management development.

Organization Design. The first part of the program consisted in developing and communicating to all employees an organization chart and job descriptions that detailed each position's responsibilities and relationships to other positions. This aspect of the organizational development program was intended to help employees understand their own jobs, others' jobs, and the relationship between their job and others' jobs. It would help them begin to separate tasks they would be held accountable for from those that should be delegated to other individuals or departments. Such a division should reduce the number of employees who felt that they needed to "do everything themselves."

Strategic Planning. The strategic planning process involved determining "who the company was" (its business definition), "where it was going" (its goals and objectives), and "how it was going to get there" (action steps). A series of meetings involving employees at various levels of the organization was used to facilitate this process. Joe and other members of top management employed procedures such as use of agendas and establishment of a designated chair for each session to increase the effectiveness of the meetings.

The first step in the strategic planning process, that of establishing and formalizing the company's identity, helped employees begin to understand the direction the company was taking and their roles in its development. This clarification reduced some of the insecurity that employees had previously felt.

The second step in the strategic planning process involved designing procedures for setting, monitoring, and evaluating financial and nonfinancial goals. The emphasis in formulating financial goals was to be on planning both sales and expenses in order to increase profit. Procedures were developed to provide managers with monthly budgets and sales figures so that they could monitor performance as progress toward goals and make changes as necessary. These procedures were intended to help the firm make the transition from a sales to a profit orientation.

Formalization of the strategic planning process was intended to help employees use their time more efficiently. This was accomplished by teaching employees how to set realistic financial and nonfinancial goals and how to develop contingency plans to be used in emergencies. Individuals were told that they would be held accountable for the accomplishment of only their own goals and helped to understand what their own and others' responsibilities were. The strategic planning process thus reduced the amount of time individuals needed to spend "putting out fires" or unnecessarily duplicating others' work.

Management Development. A third major goal of the organizational development program was to increase the effectiveness of current managers and develop a pool of qualified potential managers. To accomplish this goal, a formal management development program was created. This program consisted of lectures, exercises, and discussions designed to help participants develop the skills necessary to be effective leaders. These skills included the ability to delegate, make decisions effectively, and choose an effective leadership style.

Making the Transition: Phase IV

Joe McBride wanted to be sure that the changes brought about by the organizational development program would have a positive impact on his company's performance. He therefore established a system to monitor the program's progress in accomplishing its goals (phase IV). By monitoring the program, Joe was able to change it whenever he determined that it was no longer successful at meeting its goals or whenever employee resistance to the changes being implemented became too great.

Summary

In order to make the transition from an entrepreneurship to a professionally managed firm, a company must first recognize that such a change is needed and then design and implement a program that will facilitate the required transition. This introduction has presented a case study of one firm that was successful in making the transition.

Through the four-step program just described, Joe McBride was able to help his company begin to make a successful transition from an entrepreneurship to a professionally managed firm. The problems Joe encountered and the steps he took to overcome them were not unique to Custom Printing Corporation. In fact, Joe's experience is typical of many entrepreneurs who find that their firms have somehow "outgrown" their structures and operating systems. Joe was able to recognize these organizational growing pains and work to resolve them before it was too late.

As you will see in this book, such "organizational growing pains" occur in many entrepreneurships that reach a stage of development where a transition is needed. The methods that Joe's company used to resolve these problems have been used elsewhere and have proven quite successful.

Our introductory case study has provided you with an overview of this book. In Part One we will begin to examine in detail the way to make the transition from an entrepreneurship to a professionally managed firm.

PART I

A Framework
for Developing
Successful Organizations

The First Challenge for Entrepreneurs

The first challenge entrepreneurs face is the challenge of establishing a successful new venture. The basic skills necessary to meet this challenge are the ability to recognize a market need and the ability to develop (or hire other people to develop) a product or service appropriate to satisfy that need.

If these two fundamental things are done well, a fledgling enterprise is likely to experience rapid growth. At this point, whether the entrepreneur recognizes it or not, the game begins to change. The very fact of the firm's success creates its next set of problems and challenges to survival.

As a result of expanding sales, the firm's resources become stretched very thin. A seemingly perpetual and insatiable need arises for more inventory, space, equipment, people, funds, and so on. Day-to-day activities are greatly speeded up and may even take on a frenzied quality.

11

The firm's operational systems (those needed to facilitate day-to-day activities), such as marketing, production or service delivery, accounting, credit, collections, and personnel, typically are overwhelmed by the sudden surge of activity. There is little time to think, and little or no planning takes place because most plans quickly become obsolete. People become high on their own adrenalin and merely react to the rush of activity.

At this point the firm usually begins to experience some, perhaps all, of the following "organizational growing pains":

- People feel there are not enough hours in the day;
- People spend too much time "putting out fires";
- Many people are not aware of what others are doing;
- People lack an understanding of the firm's ultimate goals;
- There are not enough good managers;
- People feel that "I have to do it myself if I want to get it done correctly";
- Most people feel that the firm's meetings are a waste of time;
- Plans are seldom made and even more seldom followed up, so things often don't get done;
- Some people feel insecure about their place in the firm; and
- The firm has continued to grow in sales but not to the same extent in profits.

The CEO or founder must recognize these symptoms as a warning to take immediate corrective action before the firm gets into serious difficulty.

The Second Challenge for Entrepreneurs

When this stage of development is reached, the firm must prepare to make a fundamental transformation or metamorphosis from the spontaneous, *ad hoc,* free-spirited enterprise that it has been to a more formally planned, organized, and disciplined entity. The firm must move from a situation in which there are only informal plans and people simply react to events to one in which formal planning is a way of life; from one in which jobs and responsibilities are undefined to one in which there is some degree of definition of responsibilities and mutually exclusive roles; from one in which there is no accountability or control system to one in which there are goals, standards, measures, and related rewards specified in advance as well as formal performance appraisal; from one in which there is only on-the-job-training to one in which there are formal management development programs; from one in which there is no budget to one in which there are budgets, reports, and variances; and, finally, from a situation in which profit simply happens to one in which there is an explicit profit goal to be achieved. In brief, the firm must make the transition from an entrepreneurship to a professionally managed organization.

As we will see in Chapter Eleven, this is a time when the very personality traits that made the founder-entrepreneur so successful initially can lead to organizational demise. Most entrepreneurs have either a sales or a technical background, or they know a particular industry well. Entrepreneurs typically want things done in their own way. They may be more intelligent or have better intuition than their subordinates, who come to rely on their bosses' omnipotence. Typical entrepreneurs tend to be "doers" rather than managers, and most have not had formal management training, although they may read the current management best-sellers. They like to be free of "corporate constraints." They reject meetings, written plans, detailed organization of time, and budgets as the trappings of bureaucracy. Most insidiously, they think, "We got here without these things, so why do we need them?"

Unfortunately, at the stage of corporate development we are discussing, the nature of the organization has changed—and so must the firm's senior management. The owner-entrepreneur can deal with the situation in one of five different ways:

- Try to develop new skills and behavior patterns—difficult but quite possible;
- Resign, as Jack Tramiel did at Commodore International, and let others bring in a professional manager to run the organization;
- Move up to chairperson, as Steven Jobs did at Apple Computer, and bring in a professional manager while still staying involved;

- Continue to operate as before and ignore the problems, hoping they will evaporate; or
- Sell out and start another entrepreneurial company, as did K. M. Siegal, the entrepreneur who founded Conductron, sold it to McDonnell Douglas, and then started KMS Industries.

Founder-entrepreneurs typically experience great difficulty in relinquishing control of their businesses. Some try to change their skills and behavior but fail. Others merely give the illusion of turning the organization over to professional managers. For example, one successful entrepreneur brought two very highly paid and experienced managers into his firm, made a great flourish about the transition, and then proceeded to turn them into "managerial eunuchs." After they had "failed," he was able to "reluctantly" resume control of the enterprise and plead that he had made every effort but the business obviously could not do without him.

There is no one pattern for a successful transition from an entrepreneurship to a professional firm. Whatever path is followed, the key to a successful change is for the entrepreneur to recognize that a new stage in the organization's life cycle has been reached and that the former mode of operation will no longer be effective.

Making an Organizational Transition

Once the entrepreneur has recognized that the company's mode of operation must be changed, the inevitable question arises: "What should we do to take the organization successfully to the next stage of growth?" To answer this question satisfactorily, it is necessary to understand that there are predictable stages of organizational growth, certain key developmental tasks that must be performed by the organization at each growth stage, and certain critical problems that organizations typically face as they grow. This understanding, in turn, requires a framework within which the determinants of successful organizational development may be placed. We will present such a framework in Part One of this book.

Chapter One presents a holistic framework for successful organizational development. It deals with the issue of what makes an organization successful and profitable. Drawing on research and experience from consulting with many organizations, it presents a systematic approach to understanding the six critical variables in organizational effectiveness. It examines the six critical tasks of organizational development and tells what must be done to accomplish each. These six variables or tasks are conceptualized as a "pyramid of organizational development."

Chapter Two identifies four different stages of organizational growth, from the inception of a new venture through the early maturity of an entrepreneurial organization. It examines the relative emphasis that must be placed on each of the six critical developmental tasks at each stage of the organization's growth.

Chapter Three examines the growing pains that all developing organizations experience. It provides a method for assessing these growing pains and determining their severity. Senior managers need to be able to recognize such growing pains as symptoms of the need to make changes in their organizations.

Taken together, the ideas in Chapters One, Two, and Three provide a conceptual map of the tasks that must be done to manage and develop an entrepreneurial organization. Part One also provides a guide for analyzing and planning the transitions that must be made in moving a company from one developmental stage to the next.

1

How to Build
Successful Companies:
The Pyramid
of Organizational
Development

The senior management of a rapidly growing entrepreneurial company must simultaneously cope with its endless day-to-day problems and keep an eye on its future direction. Furthermore, the managers of most such companies are going through the process of building a company for the first time. This is about as easy as navigating uncharted waters in a leaky rowboat with an inexperienced crew while surrounded by a school of sharks. The sea is unfamiliar, the boat is clumsy, the skills needed are not readily apparent or not fully developed, and there is a constant reminder of the high costs of an error in judgment.

Just as the crew of such a boat might wish urgently for a guide to help them with navigation, training, and ship repair, the senior managers of an entrepreneurial company may frequently wish for a guide to help them build their firm. The crew might also be glad to know that others before them have made the voyage successfully and to hear some of the lessons that the other voyagers learned in the process.

This chapter attempts to provide a guide for senior managers who are faced with the special challenge of building an entrepreneurial company. It gives a framework for understanding and managing the critical tasks that an organization must perform at each stage of its growth.

Six Key Organizational Development Tasks

Organizational development is the process of planning and implementing changes in the overall capabilities of an enterprise in order to increase its operating effectiveness and profitability. It involves thinking about a business organization (or any organization, for that matter) as a whole and planning necessary changes in certain key areas. Proper organizational development allows entrepreneurial firms to progress successfully from one stage of growth to the next.

The framework for organizational development of entrepreneurial firms that is presented in this chapter is an outgrowth of several years of research and experience in working with such organizations. It includes six organizational development areas or tasks that are critical in determining whether an organization will be successful at any particular stage of growth. Taken together, these six key tasks comprise the "pyramid of organizational development" pictured in Figure 1. We will first identify and describe each key organizational development task individually and then examine the pyramid of organizational development as a whole.

Identify and Define a Market Niche. The most fundamental prerequisite for developing a successful organization is the identification and definition of a firm's market and, if feasible, its "market niche." A market is made up of the present and potential buyers of the goods and/or services that a firm intends to produce and sell. A market niche is a place within a market where a firm can potentially develop a competitive advantage in providing goods and/or services to satisfy customer needs.

The first challenge to organizational survival or success is identifying a market need for a good or service to which the firm will seek to respond. This can be either a need that has not yet been

Figure 1. Pyramid of Organizational Development.

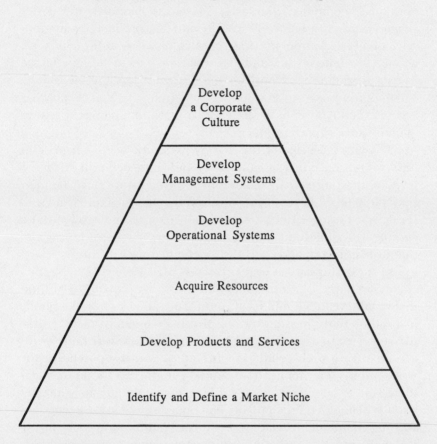

recognized by other firms or a need currently satisfied by existing firms. The chances for organizational success are enhanced if a firm identifies a need that is not being adequately fulfilled or that has little competition for its fulfillment. This challenge is faced by all new ventures; indeed, it is *the* challenge for a new venture to overcome. It has also been the critical test of many growing concerns and has even brought many once proud and great firms to near ruin or total demise.

Many firms have achieved great success merely because they were one of the first in a new market. For example, Apple Computer grew from a small entrepreneurship in a garage to a $1 billion firm in a few years because its founders identified the market for a "personal" computer. Similarly, Dreyer's, a manufacturer of ice cream (which is a relatively undifferentiated product), went from sales of $14.4 million in 1978 to sales of $55.8 million in 1982 because the company saw and cultivated a market niche between the "super-premium ice creams" such as Haagen-Dazs and the generic (commodity) ice cream sold in most supermarkets. Pic 'N' Save has become a company of more than $235 million in revenues by selling manufacturer's excess products.

The reverse side of this happy picture is seen in firms that have foundered either because they failed to define a niche or because they mistakenly abandoned their historical niche. For example, a medium-sized national firm that manufactured and sold specialty clothing wished to upgrade its image and products and become a high-fashion boutique. However, it failed to recognize that its historical market was the "medium" market, and its efforts to rise out of this market were unsuccessful.

Similarly, a printing company with more than $10 million in annual revenues found itself in difficulty after trying to upgrade its position in the medium-priced printing market. Attracted by the market segment where the highest-quality work was done (with accompanying high profit margins), the company purchased the best equipment available. It also hired a high-priced sales manager to recruit a sales force that could compete in the new market segment. However, the company had underestimated the strength of existing companies in that market niche, and it found itself unable to break into the higher-priced market segment as easily as its managers had hoped. Moreover, the additional investments it had made and the related increases in its overhead made the firm's cost structure higher than that of its former competitors, so it began losing business from its historical market niche. Thus the company found itself in a cost-price squeeze.

Many firms are able to survive merely because they have been able to identify a market need for certain goods or services; however, the firms that achieve the greatest success frequently have identified not only a market need but also a potential niche to capture. For example, Bud Knapp, Chairman of Knapp Communications Corporation, perceived a niche for magazines geared to the relatively affluent consumer and proceeded to capture that niche with *Architectural Digest.*

The first task in developing a successful organization, then, is the definition of the firm's markets and potential niches. This process involves the use of strategic market planning to identify potential customers, their needs, and so on. It also involves laying out the strategy through which the firm plans to compete with others for its share of the intended market. The nature and methods of strategic planning will be described in Chapter Seven.

Develop Products and Services. The second task of an entrepreneurial organization is "productization." This is the process of analyzing the needs of present and potential customers in order to design products and/or services that will satisfy their needs. For example, one group of entrepreneurs in the electronics industry identified the need for a solution to the so-called "backup problem" facing users of micro- and minicomputers. Such users needed a relatively inexpensive method of backing up the data on the disks used in their computers. This group of engineering-oriented entrepreneurs researched and developed a solution to the backup problem that used the technology called "tape streaming." The result was a business that began to earn more than $30 million in annual revenues in just a few years.

Although many firms are able to correctly perceive a market need, they are not necessarily able to develop a product that is capable of satisfying that need adequately. For example, the firms of California's "Silicon Valley" were able to identify the need for a 64K computer chip but the market for that product ultimately came to be dominated by Japanese companies and Motorola because of these companies' ability to mass produce the chip with a high degree of reliability. Thus, being the first to recognize a need is not necessarily sufficient.

The productization process involves not only the ability to design a "product" (defined here to include services as well) but also the ability to produce it. For a service firm, the ability to "produce" a product involves the firm's service delivery system, the mechanism through which services are provided to customers.

Productization is not simply a task for relatively new or small companies; it faces large, well-established firms as well. Indeed, it can even face whole industries. For example, in the 1970s U.S. automobile manufacturers were unsuccessful in productizing their products to meet the changing needs of their market, including the growing need for reliable, fuel-efficient, economical automobiles. As a result, Japan emerged as a powerful competitor in a market that the Americans had once dominated.

The development of successful products depends to a great extent on effective strategic market planning. This involves understanding who your potential customers are, what their needs are, how they buy, and what they perceive to be value in a product.

The success of productization depends, to a very great extent, on success in defining the firm's market niche. The greater the degree to which a firm understands the market's needs, the more likely that its productization process will be effective in satisfying those needs. Productization is the second key development task in building a successful organization.

Acquire Resources. The third major task of a developing organization is acquiring and developing the additional resources it needs for its present and anticipated future growth. A firm may have identified a market and created products but not have sufficient resources to compete effectively. For example, small competitors in the soft drink industry need to be low-cost producers. This requires high-speed bottling lines, which, at a cost of $1 million a line, the smaller firms simply cannot afford.

A firm's success in identifying a market niche and in productization creates increased demand for its products and/or services. This, in turn, stretches the firm's resources very thin. The organization may suddenly find that it requires additional physical resources (space, equipment, and so on), financial resources, and human resources. The need for human resources, especially in management, will become particularly acute. At this stage of development, the firm's very success ironically creates a new set of problems.

The company must now become more adept at resource management, including the management of cash, inventories (if a manufacturing company), personnel, and so forth. It is at this stage that an entrepreneur must begin to think in longer terms about the company's future needs. Failure to do this can be costly. For example, one entrepreneur told how he kept purchasing equipment that became obsolete for the company's needs within six months because of the firm's rapid growth. Instead of purchasing a photocopying machine that would be adequate for the company's needs as it grew but was more than currently required, for example, he purchased a machine that was able to meet only current needs. The result was that he spent much more on equipment than he would have done if he had purchased machinery that was adequate for potential future needs. Similarly, another entrepreneur found himself with insufficient space six months after moving into new offices that he had thought would be adequate for five years, because the company grew more rapidly than he had anticipated.

Develop Operational Systems. To function effectively, a firm must not only produce a product or service but also administer basic day-to-day operations reasonably well. These operations include accounting, billing, collections, advertising, personnel recruiting and training, sales, production, delivery, and related systems. The fourth task in building a successful organization is the development of the systems needed to facilitate these day-to-day operations—the operational systems. It is useful to think of a firm's operational systems as part of its "organizational plumbing." Just as plumbing is necessary for a house or building to function effectively, organizational plumbing is necessary for a business to function well.

Typically, firms that are busy developing their market niche and products tend to neglect the development of their operational systems. As a firm increases in size, however, an increasing amount of strain is put on such systems because the company tends to outgrow the organizational plumbing available to operate it.

For example, in one electrical components distribution firm with more than $200 million in annual revenues, salespeople were continually infuriated when they found that deliveries of products they had sold could not be made because the firm's inventory records were hopelessly incorrect. Similarly, a medium-sized residential real estate firm with annual revenues of about $10 million found that it required almost one year of effort and embarrassment to correct its accounting records after the firm's bookkeeper retired. A $100 million consumer products manufacturer had to return certain materials to vendors because it had insufficient warehouse space to house the purchases (a fact no one noticed until the deliveries were at the door). A $15 million industrial abrasives distributor found itself facing constant problems in keeping track of customer orders and in knowing what was in its inventory. The firm's inventory control system, which was fine when annual sales were $3 to $5 million, had simply become overloaded at the higher sales volume. One manager remarked that "nothing is ever stored around here where any intelligent person could reasonably expect to find it."

Develop Management Systems. The fifth task required to build a successful organization is developing the management systems required for the long-run growth and development of the firm. These include systems for planning, organization, management development, and control. Management systems are another component of an organization's infrastructure, or "plumbing."

The planning system takes care of planning for the overall development of the organization as well as for scheduling and budgeting operations. It involves the processes of strategic planning, operational planning, and contingency planning. A firm may do planning but still lack a planning system. The basic concepts and methods of strategic planning for entrepreneurial companies are presented in Chapter Seven.

The organization system of the firm determines how people are organized, who reports to whom, and how activities are coordinated. All firms have some organizational structure (formal or informal), but they do not necessarily have the correct structure for their needs.

The management development system sees to the planned development of the people needed to run the organization as it grows. Chapter Nine deals with management development and its role in making the transition from entrepreneurship to professional management.

The control system encompasses the set of processes (budgeting, leadership, goal setting) and mechanisms (performance appraisal) used to motivate employees to achieve organizational objectives. It includes both formal control mechanisms, such as responsibility accounting, and informal processes, such as organizational leadership. Chapter Eight deals with organizational control systems.

Until the firm reaches a certain size (which tends to differ for each firm), it can typically operate without formal management systems. Planning tends to be done in the head of the entrepreneur, frequently on an *ad hoc* basis. The organizational structure, if it exists, tends to be informal, with ill-defined responsibilities that may well overlap several people. Management development tends to consist of "on-the-job training," which basically means "You're on your own." When control systems are used in such organizations, they tend to involve only the accounting system rather than a broader concept of management control.

The basic organizational growing pain at this level of development is the decreasing ability of the original entrepreneur or senior executive to control all that is happening. The organization simply becomes too large for senior managers to be personally involved in every aspect of it.

Develop a Corporate Culture. Just as all people have personalities, all organizations have a culture: a set of shared values, beliefs, and norms that govern the way people are expected to operate the business on a day-to-day basis. The culture may be implicit rather than explicit, but it can be identified by trained observers.

Values are what the organization believes is important with respect to product quality, customer service, treatment of people, and so on. Beliefs are the ideas that people in the corporation hold about themselves as individuals and about the firm as an entity. Norms are the unwritten rules that guide day-to-day interactions and behavior, including language, dress, and humor.

Organizational culture is a critical factor in an enterprise's successful development and performance. It can have a profound impact upon the behavior of people for better or worse. Many companies have achieved greatness at least in part because of a strong corporate culture.

Some managers believe that what is espoused as their corporate culture is actually the culture that affects people's behavior. Unfortunately, this is often an illusion. For example, one rapidly growing entrepreneurship stated that its culture involved the production of high-quality products, concern for the quality of the working life of its employees, and encouragement of innovation. In reality, the firm's culture was less positive. Its true concerns were to avoid conflict among its managers, set unrealistic performance expectations, avoid accountability, and overestimate its performance capabilities. Moreover, the company saw itself as hard-driving and profit oriented, but its real culture was sales-oriented regardless of profitability.

Sophisticated managers understand that their companies compete as much with culture as with specific products and services. The CEO of a major New York Stock Exchange company once said that he could predict a division's organizational problems as soon as he had identified its culture. The sixth and final challenge in building a successful organization, then, is to develop and institutionalize the corporate culture.

The Pyramid of Organizational Development

The six tasks of organizational development just described are critical to a firm's successful functioning, not only individually but as an integrated structure. They must comprise an organizational system, harmonizing and reinforcing rather than conflicting with one another. When they function effectively together, the six key tasks of organizational development make up a "pyramid of organizational development." The management of an organization must learn to visualize this pyramid and evaluate their organization in terms of the extent to which its pyramid has been successfully designed and built.

We must also recognize that although an organization always contains the pyramid of systems that deal with the six key developmental tasks, the emphasis on the components or subsystems of the pyramid must be somewhat different at different stages of organizational growth. Before we can explore this idea further, we must examine the different stages of growth through which entrepreneurial organizations develop. This topic will be the focus of Chapter Two. First, however, let us examine an example of the building of the pyramid of organizational development at a successful company.

Successfully Building the Pyramid: The Example of IBM

International Business Machines Corporation (IBM) is a classic example of an organization that has been successful in building its pyramid of organizational development. It has achieved success in handling the six critical tasks of developing an effective organization not only individually but as a whole. Although IBM is much larger than the entrepreneurial organizations we are concerned with in this book, taking a closer look at what it has done can still be instructive. For one thing, even IBM was once a fledgling new venture. For another, IBM has demonstrated that even a company with sales exceeding $40 billion can act entrepreneurially, as it did when it introduced its PC computer.

Identify a Market Niche and Develop a Product. At its core, IBM is a market-driven company. It does not regard marketing merely in the narrow sense of sales and advertising; rather, it focuses on the market and market needs in the ways described in our discussion of the first two levels of the pyramid framework. Specifically, the company is concerned with identifying present and potential customer needs and then developing products to satisfy those needs. Although IBM has a reputation for product quality, the company's strategy is not to bring products to market that are of the highest possible intrinsic quality; rather, IBM prides itself on its ability to develop profitable products that are of the quality level that customers desire (that is, will purchase). While a Televideo computer may be a more technologically sophisticated machine with a more powerful chip, the IBM PC has become the dominant product in its market. Thus, one of the central tenets of the company's orientation is the satisfaction of customer needs. This is symbolized in the organization's culture as a concern for "customer service," but in reality it is broader than that phrase would suggest.

Acquire Resources and Develop Operational Systems.
Unlike many entrepreneurial companies, even those with sales in
excess of $1 billion, IBM has paid a great deal of attention to the
next two levels of the pyramid of organizational development. The
company has developed its resources and operational systems so
that it has the operational infrastructure (organizational plumbing)
to run efficiently and effectively on a day-to-day basis. The company
takes as much pride in the excellence of its people, plant,
equipment, and operational systems as it does in its products. This
attitude, in turn, is based upon the company's belief in its own
excellence and in excellence as a criterion to evaluate its own
performance. While many companies strive for excellence in their
products or services, relatively few strive for excellence in all that
they do. IBM is one of the exceptions.

Develop Management Systems. IBM has also developed an
outstanding set of management systems, including systems for
strategic and operational planning, management development,
organization, and control. The company's comprehensive strategic
planning system includes environmental scanning capability to
identify and assess the implications of long-term trends. IBM also
has a well-developed profit planning and budgeting system. All of
IBM's planning is done on a regularly scheduled annual basis.

IBM's management development system and practices are
one of the truly outstanding parts of its management system. IBM
has invested heavily in management development, and it attributes
much of its long-term success to this practice. The company
requires that each manager go through what amounts to "basic
management training" within thirty days of becoming a manager.
Moreover, each manager must have forty hours of management
development training each year. IBM uses the mechanism of
management development not only to develop managerial skills but
also to institutionalize the organization's culture.

Organization of a company as large and complex as IBM is
a considerable challenge, yet the company is well organized and
functions effectively. The basic concept behind IBM's organization
is decentralization with control. The company is organized into
relatively autonomous divisions, all of which are coordinated and
subject to centralized guidance and control. It is not merely a

collection of loosely affiliated operating entities under a holding company management structure, like Beatrice Foods; rather, it is an integrated organization with a balance between centralized planning and review and autonomous day-to-day decision making.

The company's control systems consist of an extensive reporting system plus periodic meetings for performance review. The company also monitors a number of variables over time to assess trends and deviations that may indicate problems. Finally, IBM has a well-developed performance appraisal system.

Develop a Corporate Culture. The highest level in the pyramid of organizational development is the corporate culture. Throughout its history, IBM has been aware of the role of corporate culture in the management of its organization. Under Thomas Watson, the firm formulated a set of three critical values that still persist today. These are customer service, excellence of performance, and respect for the individual.

Customer service, which has already been described in connection with the company's marketing orientation, is a broader concept than merely providing customer satisfaction. It comes closer to meaning a total commitment to understanding and trying to serve customer needs.

The concept of excellence has also been described briefly. It seems to be best captured by the phrase of one IBMer that "we try to do things the right way." When mistakes are made (and IBM, just like any other company, does make mistakes), people "swarm" over the problem to find its causes and correct it.

Finally, the company's notion of "respect for the individual" needs to be understood as something more than that phrase might imply. IBM's concern for its employees is not necessarily a selfless, humanistic concern, but it is a concern nonetheless. In spite of having hundreds of thousands of employees, IBM continues to operate within a culture that stresses the dignity and worth of each individual. The company has an open-door policy and practices that make it feasible for the individual to be heard. It assigns personnel officers to each operating division to serve as advisors on human resource issues to operating management. The company runs an annual morale survey to get feedback from people concerning their satisfaction with work-related issues. The IBM value of respect for the individual involves an implied reciprocity between the company and its employees: If employees will commit themselves to taking care of the company, the company will take care of them.

The Pyramid as a Whole. IBM's management fully realizes that the six key development factors are not only important in themselves; they constitute a system. IBM seems to be managed as a holistic entity made up of interacting, mutually reinforcing systems. The company provides an outstanding illustration of an enterprise that has successfully achieved its pyramid of organizational development.

Summary

This chapter has presented a framework for understanding what makes an organization successful, effective, and profitable. The framework includes six key areas in which organizations must succeed: (1) markets, (2) products or services, (3) resources, (4) operational systems, (5) management systems, and (6) corporate culture. For organizations to be successful, they must deal not only with each of these six areas individually and in sequence but also with the six as parts of a whole. We use the image of a "pyramid of organizational development" to describe this holistic approach.

IBM illustrates the power of developing a company in a way that is consistent with the pyramid of organizational development. However, companies need not be large like IBM in order to be able to do what IBM has done. In fact, the larger the company, the greater the difficulty in achieving a successful pyramid of development.

An organization does not have to be a billion-dollar company before a pyramid of organizational development is complete; a version of the pyramid exists at all different stages of organizational growth. The different stages of growth and the different emphasis on each part of the pyramid that is required at each growth stage will be the subject of the next chapter.

2

⦇⦈⦉⦊ ⦇⦈⦉⦊ ⦇⦈⦉⦊

Identifying and Surviving
the Four Major Stages
of Organizational Growth

All organizations pass through various stages of development. These stages are, at least in part, determined by the organization's size, as measured by its annual revenues. This chapter presents a framework for identifying and explaining the major stages through which all organizations grow and develop as they increase in size.*

First, we will describe the various stages of organizational growth, from the inception of a new venture to organizational maturity. Next, we will examine the emphasis on each level in the pyramid of organizational development that is required at each growth stage and explain the nature of the transitions to different stages. We will also examine the stages of growth that occur after organizational maturity. Finally, we will discuss some implications of this framework for the management of entrepreneurial organizations.

Stages of Organizational Growth

Four stages of growth for a firm on its way to organizational maturity can be identified:

*It should be noted that this framework applies to a division of a large company as well as to an independent organization.

1.   New venture;
2.   Expansion;
3.   Professionalization; and
4.   Consolidation.

At each of these stages, one or more of the critical tasks of organizational development should receive special attention. The stages of organizational growth, the critical development areas for each stage, and the approximate size (measured in millions of dollars of sales revenues) at which an organization will pass through each stage are shown in Table 1.

Stage I: New Venture. Stage I of organizational growth involves the inception of a new venture. Stage I typically occurs from the time an organization has virtually no sales until it reaches approximately $1 million in annual sales. During stage I, the firm has to perform all the critical tasks necessary for organizational success, but the greatest emphasis is on the first two tasks: defining markets and developing products. This is represented schematically in the organizational development pyramid shown in Figure 2. Those two tasks are the tasks of survival.

Table 1. Stages of Organizational Growth.

Stage No.	Description	Critical Development Areas	Approximate Organizational Size (Millions of Dollars in Sales)
I.	New venture	Markets and products	Less than $1
II.	Expansion	Resources and operational systems	$1 to $10
III.	Professionalization	Management systems	$10 to $100
IV.	Consolidation	Corporate culture	$100 to $500

Figure 2. Developmental Emphasis in a Stage I Firm.

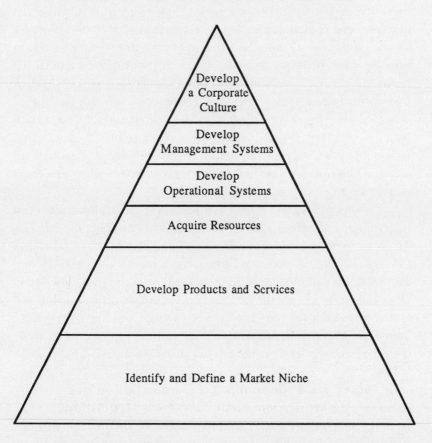

Many firms have succeeded in establishing new ventures because the entrepreneur was able to identify a viable market and product. Earl Scheib, the "king of the no-frills auto paint job," is one entrepreneur who met this challenge. When he began painting cars in his Los Angeles gas station in 1937, his original concept was to provide a no-frills face-lift for cars. Scheib built an entire business based upon this concept. He had successfully identified a market niche that was not being served, and he proceeded to build a business to serve it. His company is now publicly held and in 1985 operated more than 275 shops for paint and bodywork on cars. Moreover, his concept has been copied by a number of competitors.

Another example of an entrepreneur who established a successful new venture because he was able to identify an unserved market niche is Thomas S. Monaghan, who founded the company known today as Domino's Pizza. Monaghan's concept was to provide pizza for home delivery, which at the time he founded his business was not commonly available. As he has stated: "When Domino's began delivering pizza, the only pizza places that delivered were those that had to deliver to survive."* Monaghan believed that there was an unserved market need for high-quality, reasonably priced pizza to be delivered to the home. Today his firm serves approximately one-half of the home delivery pizza market, a market Domino's Pizza helped create.

Other examples of new ventures that came about when an entrepreneur perceived a market niche to be served include Famous Amos Cookies, Federal Express Corp., and Kinder Care Day Care Centers as well as Ashton-Tate, which markets dBASE II and dBASE III, popular database management software packages. Many other new ventures are reasonably successful and profitable but not as famous. They include businesses engaged in executive search, landscape design, printing, financial planning, restaurants, graphic design, repair services, catering, equipment leasing, and many more fields.

Stage II: Expansion. If an organization successfully completes the key developmental tasks of stage I, it will reach stage II. This stage involves the rapid expansion of the firm in terms of sales revenues, number of employees, and so on. For most firms, stage II begins at about the $1 million sales level and extends to the $10 million level.

Stage II presents a new set of developmental problems and challenges. Organizational resources are stretched to the limit when increasing sales require a seemingly endless increase in people, financing, equipment, and space. Similarly, the firm's day-to-day operational systems for recruiting, production or service delivery, purchasing, accounting, collections, and payables are nearly

* "Starting Small and Growing Big: The Essentials of Managing Growth," *Dividend*, Winter 1983, p. 8.

overwhelmed by the sheer amount of product or service being "pushed out the door."

The major problems that occur during stage II are problems of growth rather than survival. It is during this stage that "horror stories" begin to accumulate:

- Salespeople sell a product they know is in inventory, only to learn that someone else has grabbed it for other customers.
- One vendor's invoices are paid two and three times, while another vendor hasn't been paid in six months.
- A precipitous drop in product quality occurs for unknown reasons.
- Turnover increases sharply just when the company needs more personnel.
- Missing letters, files, and reports cause confusion, loss of time, and embarrassment.
- Senior executives find themselves scheduled to be in two widely separated cities on the same day at the same time, or they arrive in a distant city only to learn that they are a day early.

Organizational growing pains typical of a stage II company will be discussed in detail in Chapter Three. The relative emphasis on each key developmental task appropriate for stage II is shown schematically in Figure 3.

Many companies experience a great deal of difficulty during stage II and may even disappear. When this occurs, it is usually because the founding entrepreneur is unable to cope with the managerial problems that arise as the organization grows. A stage II company needs an infrastructure of operational systems that lets it operate efficiently and effectively on a day-to-day basis. Unfortunately, many entrepreneurs are not interested in such "organizational plumbing."

Some firms that are fortunate enough to have discovered an especially rich market niche find themselves growing very rapidly. Although most development of a firm's resources and operational systems ought to occur during the period when the firm is growing from $1 million to $10 million in annual revenues, it is not unusual

Figure 3. Developmental Emphasis in a Stage II Firm.

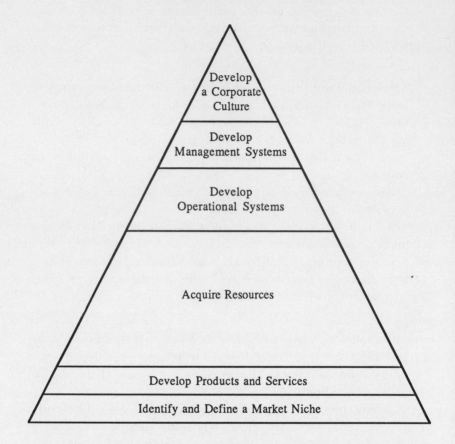

to find firms with $30, $40, $50, and even more than $100 million in annual revenues with the operational systems of a stage II company. This kind of discrepancy between a firm's size and the degree of development of its operational systems leads to serious problems, but these may be masked in the short term by the firm's rapidly rising revenues. This often proves to be the case in the most spectacular examples of organizational failure, such as Osborne Computer Corporation. In an article on the rise and fall of Adam Osborne, Steve Coll states, "In retrospect, it seems clear that the company's accounting procedures were so slipshod that no one knew how things were."* Chapter Four will present several examples of companies that were successful at stages I and II but experienced developmental problems during their transitions.

Taken together, stages I and II, the new venture and expansion stages, constitute the entrepreneurial phase of organizational development. It is during these two stages of growth that the classic skills of entrepreneurship are most relevant. It is also during this phase that the need to make the transition from an entrepreneurial to a professionally managed organization begins to occur.

Stage III: Professionalization. Somewhere during the period of explosive growth that characterizes stage II, senior management realizes (or ought to realize) that a need for a qualitative change in the firm is arising. The company cannot merely add people, money, equipment, and space to cope with its growth; it must undergo a transition or metamorphosis and become a somewhat different type of organization, as illustrated in the Custom Printing example described in the Introduction.

Until this point, the firm has been entrepreneurial. It has operated with a considerable degree of informality. It may have lacked well-defined goals, responsibilities, plans, or controls but still prospered. However, once a critical size has been achieved, many of these practices and procedures must be increasingly formalized. The need for this transition typically occurs by the time an organization has reached approximately $10 million in sales. The sheer size of the organization then requires more formal plans, regularly scheduled meetings, defined organizational roles and responsibilities, a performance appraisal system, and management control systems. These in turn require a planned program of organizational development.

The people who manage the firm must also change their skills and capabilities. Until this point, it was possible to be more of a doer or hands-on manager than a professional manager. At this stage, however, the organization increasingly requires people who

*Steve Coll, "The Rise and Fall of Adam Osborne," *California Magazine*, November 1983, p. 92.

are adept at formal administration, planning, organization, motivation, leadership, and control.

The relative emphasis on each key developmental task appropriate for stage III is shown schematically in Figure 4. As the figure indicates, the most important task during this stage is the development of management systems.

Although the professionalization of a firm ought to occur during the period when sales are growing from $10 million to approximately $100 million, the rate of corporate growth often outstrips the rate at which the enterprise's management systems are

Figure 4. Developmental Emphasis in a Stage III Firm.

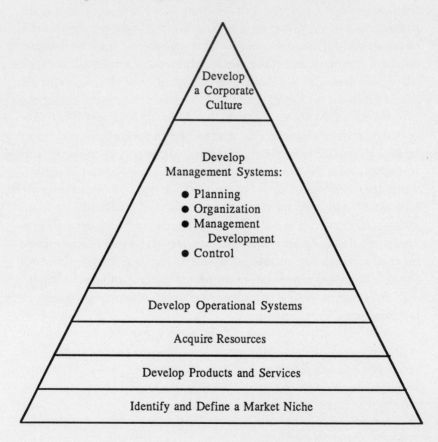

developed. This can lead to serious problems. An example of these problems can be seen in Apple Computer. Apple is essentially a stage II company in the process of making the transition to stage III, even though its corporate revenues in 1984 were about $2 billion.

Chapter Five will present the case history of one organization that made the transition from stage II to stage III successfully. It will examine the process through which this transition was accomplished and the problems that were encountered along the way.

Stage IV: Consolidation. Once an organization has made the transition to a professionally managed firm with workable systems for planning, organization, management, development, and control, the firm must turn its attention to an intangible but nevertheless real and significant asset: the corporate culture. Development of a corporate culture is the main task of stage IV of organizational development.

Corporate culture can have a powerful effect not only on day-to-day operations but on the bottom line of profitability as well. During the growth that was necessary to reach stage IV (which typically seems to begin at about $100 million in sales), the firm has brought in new "waves" of people. The first wave probably arrived when the firm was relatively small and informal, during stage I. During this period, the firm's culture (values, beliefs, and norms) was transmitted by direct day-to-day contact between the founder(s) and personnel. The diffusion or transmission of culture was a by-product of what the firm did. Virtually everybody knew everybody else. Everybody also knew what the firm wanted to achieve and how.

During stage II, the rapid expansion of the firm most likely brought in a second wave of people. The first-wave personnel transmitted the corporate culture to this new generation. However, at an increased level of organizational size, especially once the firm develops geographically separate operations, this informal socialization process becomes more attenuated and less effective. The sheer number of new people simply overwhelms the socialization system.

By the time a firm reaches $100 million in revenues, a third wave of people usually has joined the organization, and the informal socialization system is no longer adequate to do what it once did so well. At this stage, the firm must develop a more conscious and formal method of transmitting the corporate culture throughout the organization. Many companies are currently trying to reshape their corporate culture in this way. Chapter Six will present the case history of one organization that is in the process of changing its corporate culture as it makes the transition to stage IV.

The relative emphasis on each key developmental task appropriate for stage IV is pictured in Figure 5.

Differences Between Entrepreneurial and Professional Management

Stages I and II, taken together, make up the entrepreneurial phase of organizational development, while stages III and IV make up the professional management phase. As an organization passes from one of these phases of growth to the other, a variety of changes will occur in it.

There is a qualitative difference between an entrepreneurship and a professionally managed organization. The former tends to be characterized by informality, lack of systems, and a free-spirited nature. The latter tends to be more formal, to have well-developed systems, and to be proud of its disciplined, profit-oriented approach.

The most important differences between an entrepreneurship and a professionally managed organization involve nine key "result areas": (1) profit, (2) planning, (3) organization, (4) control, (5) management development, (6) budgeting, (7) innovation, (8) leadership, and (9) culture. Table 2 summarizes the principal characteristics of professional management as compared with entrepreneurial management in each of these key result areas. We will now describe these differences in greater detail.

Profit. In a professionally managed firm, profit is an explicit goal; it is planned, rather than a residual, or whatever is left over at the end of the year. In an entrepreneurial firm, profit is sought,

Figure 5. Developmental Emphasis in a Stage IV Firm.

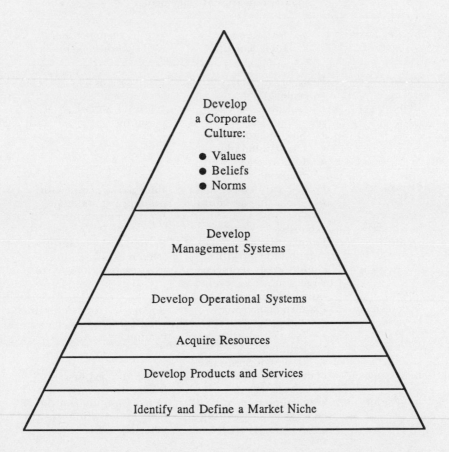

Develop
a Corporate
Culture:

● Values
● Beliefs
● Norms

Develop
Management Systems

Develop Operational Systems

Acquire Resources

Develop Products and Services

Identify and Define a Market Niche

but it is not an explicit goal to be attained. The entrepreneur(s) may be willing to invest and sacrifice current profits for a future "big hit."

Planning. A professionally managed firm has a formal, written business plan. Planning becomes a way of life, and the firm begins to develop a strategic plan for what it wants to become as well as operational plans at all levels of the company. Contingency or "what if" plans also are developed. The practice of informal,

Table 2. Comparison of Professional Management and
Entrepreneurial Management.

Key Result Areas	Professional Management	Entrepreneurial Management
Profit	Profit orientation; profit is an explicit goal.	Profit seen as a by-product.
Planning	Formal, systematic planning: • Strategic planning • Operational planning • Contingency planning.	Informal, *ad hoc* planning.
Organization	Formal, explicit role descriptions that are mutually exclusive and exhaustive.	Informal structure with overlapping and undefined responsibilities.
Control	Formal, planned system of organizational control, including explicit objectives, targets, measures, evaluation, and rewards.	Partial, *ad hoc* control; seldom uses formal measurement.
Management Development	Planned management development: • Identification of requirements • Design of programs.	*Ad hoc* development, principally through on-the-job training.
Budgeting	Management by standards and variances.	Budget not explicit; no follow-up on variances.
Innovation	Orientation to incremental innovations; willingness to take calculated risks.	Orientation to major innovations; willingness to take major risks.
Leadership	Consultative or participative styles.	Styles may vary from very directive to laissez-faire.
Culture	Well-defined culture.	Loosely defined, "family"-oriented culture.

superficial, *ad hoc* planning is replaced by a regular planning cycle.

Organization. An entrepreneurial firm has an informal organizational structure with overlapping and undefined responsibilities. A professionally managed firm has a set of written role descriptions that clearly state responsibilities. These descriptions are designed to be mutually exclusive and exhaustive.

Control. In an entrepreneurship, control of operations tends to be lacking or at least piecemeal. The firm lacks formal measurement or performance appraisal systems. A professionally managed firm, by contrast, has a formal, planned system of organizational control. This system makes full use of explicit objectives and goals, measurements of performance, feedback, evaluation, and rewards.

Development. Management development is planned in a professionally managed firm. The firm makes a conscious effort to develop the managerial skills of individuals and to prepare a pool of managers for the firm as a whole. In an entrepreneurship, however, management development is unplanned and tends to occur, if at all, through on-the-job experience.

Budgeting. In an entrepreneurship, budgeting tends to lack detail. There is little follow-up on variances or deviations from the budget. A professionally managed firm's budget system focuses on standards and variances. Managers are held accountable for performance compared against budget goals.

Innovation. By definition, entrepreneurial companies are oriented toward innovation. Many are willing to make major innovations in products, services, or operating methods. Some entrepreneurs even "bet the company" on an innovation because of the high payoff for success. Professionally managed organizations tend to be oriented more toward incremental innovations. They are less likely to bet the company, and they often spread their risk among a portfolio of different products or projects. They are willing to take calculated risks, but they may seem relatively averse to risks, at least in comparison to entrepreneurial companies. Their results may often be less spectacular than those of entrepreneurial companies on both the up side and the down side.

Leadership. In entrepreneurial companies, leadership typically ranges from very directive styles such as autocratic or benevolent autocratic to very nondirective styles such as laissez-faire (see Chapter Ten for a discussion of different leadership styles). In a professionally managed organization, the tendency today is toward more interactive styles, such as consultative and participative management. Entrepreneurial organizations are more likely to have charismatic leaders than are professionally managed companies because of the nature of the process of selection for promotion in large organizations. Lee Iacocca is one exception.

Culture. Culture tends to be loosely defined in entrepreneurial organizations. Usually it is not explicitly managed by the firm. Often the culture of an entrepreneurial organization is oriented to a "family" feeling, which is feasible because of the firm's relatively small size. Professionally managed organizations are more likely to treat organizational culture explicitly as a variable to be managed and transmitted throughout the organization.

Relevance of Differences. Our discussion of the differences between entrepreneurial and professionally managed organizations is intended to be descriptive rather than evaluative. Both types have strengths and limitations. The significant point is that different styles are appropriate at different stages of organizational growth.

From an entrepreneurial organization's standpoint, it is clear that something inevitably will be lost as the organization makes the transition to professional management. However, something will also be gained. Just as a plant that has been successful in its pot must be transplanted if it is to continue to grow and develop properly, an organization that has outgrown its infrastructure and style of management must also make a transformation. Failure to do so will lead to a variety of problems.

Discrepancies Between Growth and Organizational Development

As we have seen, two independent dimensions are involved in each stage of organizational growth: size and the extent to which the enterprise has developed systems in each of the six critical development areas. An organization can be at stage III in terms of size, as measured in annual revenues, but only at stage II in its internal organizational capabilities. For example, after only a very few years of existence, Osborne Computer Corporation was a stage IV company in size, but it was only a stage II company in organizational development.

An organization will face significant problems if its internal development is too far out of step with its size. The greater the degree of incongruity between an organization's size and the development of its operational systems, the greater is the probability that the firm will experience organizational growing pains. Such a firm is like a thirteen-year-old boy who is well over six feel tall: he has the body of a man but, most likely, the mind of a child. As a senior manager in one organization stated: "We are essentially a $30 million company that happened to have $350 million in sales." The manager meant that the firm had the operating systems and developmental structure of a $30 million company, but its growth had given it more than ten times as much revenues. Predictably, the company was in trouble.

Managing the Transition Between Growth Stages

There are four steps by which the senior managers of a rapidly growing entrepreneurial company can assist their company to make a smooth transition from one stage of growth to the next. They are as follows:

1. Perform an organizational evaluation or audit of the company's effectiveness at its current stage of development
2. Formulate an organizational development plan
3. Implement the plan through action plans and programs
4. Monitor the programs for effectiveness.

Each of these steps will now be examined in detail.

Perform an organizational evaluation or audit. The first step in making a smooth growth transition is to apply our framework to the organization, identifying its current stage of development and its strengths and weaknesses in the six key development areas. This can be done by performing an organizational evaluation or audit in each of the key areas—a systematic assessment, by means of data analysis and interviews with organization members, of the extent to which the company's organizational systems are adequate to meet the firm's current and anticipated future requirements. An organizational evaluation may be performed by the firm's management, but many firms prefer to have independent consultants make the audit in order to obtain greater objectivity. The findings of the evaluation represent a diagnosis of the organization at its current stage of development.

Formulate an organizational development plan. Once the organizational evaluation has been completed, management must develop a master plan or blueprint for building the capabilities needed for the organization to function successfully at its current or next stage of development. This is the organizational development plan. It should include specific goals and action plans for the implementation of those goals. Typically, the first step in the planning process is strategic planning, which involves people at various organizational levels. Strategic planning will be described in Chapter Seven.

Implement the organizational development plan and monitor its progress. The third and fourth steps in preparing an organization for the transition to a new growth stage are implementing the changes set forth in the organizational development plan and monitoring their effects. This includes both developing new organizational systems (planning, organization, control) and developing management's capabilities through corporate education programs. Management development programs may focus upon administrative skills (such as planning), leadership skills, or both. We will examine the role of management development programs in a case study in Chapter Nine and describe the types of leadership skills required in Chapter Ten. Implementation of the organizational development program may also involve changes in the corporate culture.

Once the development program has been implemented, management needs to monitor its progress in meeting the developmental needs of the firm. Such monitoring allows senior managers to make changes in the program whenever they determine that it no longer meets its intended goals.

These four steps—diagnosing, planning, implementing, and monitoring changes in the organizational capabilities of a company—are the keys to making a smooth transition from an entrepreneurship to a professionally managed firm. The steps are the same regardless of the size, industry, or current stage of development of a firm.

It should be noted that these steps may appear simple, but they are often quite complex in practice. The transition process will typically require one to two years for a stage I firm, while three years or more may well be required in a stage IV firm. Some aspects of the change, such as changes in personnel (voluntary or otherwise), may be difficult to handle. However, where the process is suitably designed and well executed, the firm will almost always emerge from it stronger and more successful than ever.

Summary

This chapter has presented a framework to help senior managers understand and guide organizations at different stages of growth and development. It has described the four major stages of organizational growth, from the inception of a new venture (stage I) to the consolidation of a professionally managed firm (stage IV). It has examined the degree of emphasis that must be placed on each level of the pyramid of organizational development at each stage of growth. It has also examined the differences between an entrepreneurial and a professionally managed organization. Finally, it has described the steps that must be taken to make a successful transition from one stage of growth to the next.

In the next chapter, we will examine the nature of organizational growing pains and present a method for measuring and interpreting them. Recognition and identification of these growing pains is a necessary part of the organizational evaluation process, which is the first step of the transition from an entrepreneurship to a professionally managed firm.

3

❧❧❧ ❧❧❧ ❧❧❧

Recognizing Growing Pains
and Assessing
the Need for Change

When an organization has not been fully successful in developing the internal systems it needs at a given stage of growth, it begins to experience growing pains. This chapter examines in detail the most common organizational growing pains, showing through examples how these growing pains emerge in real-life companies. It also presents a method of measuring organizational growing pains and interpreting the extent to which they signal the need for further organizational development. Finally, it discusses the degree to which different sizes and types of business experience growing pains.

The Ten Most Common Organizational Growing Pains

As organizations enlarge, they often experience a variety of growing pains that signal that something has gone wrong in the process of organizational development. Such symptoms are especially likely to occur in a stage II company, where they warn of the need for a transition to stage III. The ten most common organizational growing pains are listed in Table 3 and described in the pages that follow.

Insufficient Hours in the Day. One of the most common organizational growning pains is the feeling that there are not

Table 3. Common Organizational Growing Pains.

1. People feel that "there are not enough hours in the day."
2. People spend too much time "putting out fires."
3. People are not aware of what other people are doing.
4. People lack understanding about where the firm is headed.
5. There are too few good managers.
6. People feel that "I have to do it myself if I want to get it done correctly."
7. Most people feel that meetings are a waste of time.
8. When plans are made, there is very little follow-up, so things just don't get done.
9. Some people feel insecure about their place in the firm.
10. The firm continues to grow in sales but not in profits.

enough hours in the day. Employees feel that they could work twenty-four hours per day, seven days a week, and still not have sufficient time to get everything done. They begin to complain about "overload" and excessive stress. Both individuals and departments feel that they are always trying to catch up but never succeeding. The more work they do, the more there seems to be, resulting in a never-ending cycle. People feel as if they were on a treadmill.

The effects of these feelings can be far reaching. First, employees' belief that they are being needlessly overworked may bring on morale problems. Complaints may increase. Second, employees may begin to experience physical illnesses brought on by excessive stress. These psychological and physical problems may lead to increased absenteeism, which can decrease the company's productivity. Finally, employees may simply decide that they can no longer operate under these conditions and may leave the organization. This will result in significant turnover costs and replacement costs related to recruiting, selecting, and training new people.

When many employees have the feeling that there is not enough time in the day, usually no one is suffering more from this feeling than the company's founding entrepreneur. The entrepreneur, feeling ultimately responsible for the firm's success, may work sixteen hours a day, seven days a week in an effort to keep the company operating effectively and help it grow. As the organization grows, the entrepreneur begins to notice that he or she can no longer exercise complete control over its functioning. This realization can result in a great deal of personal stress. We will see examples of this in the cases of Metro Realty and Tempo Products (Chapters Five and Six).

Too Much Time Spent "Putting Out Fires." A second common growing pain shows itself in excessive time spent dealing with short-term crises—"putting out fires." This problem usually results from a lack of long-range planning. Individual employees and the organization as a whole live from day-to-day, never knowing what to expect. The result may be a loss of organizational productivity, effectiveness, and efficiency.

Examples of the "putting out fires" problem are easy to find. In the case of Custom Printing, described in the Introduction, a lack of planning caused orders to be needlessly rushed, resulting in excessive pressure on employees. Drivers had to be hired on weekends and evenings to deliver orders, some of which were already overdue.

In other companies, which we will discuss in more detail later, lack of planning produced other short-term crises. At Metro Realty, for example, it resulted in shortages of salespeople. Because of these shortages, Metro was forced to hire new people and put them to work almost immediately, sometimes without adequate training. This, in turn, contributed to short-term productivity problems because the new people did not possess the skills necessary to be good salespeople. You will see that at Tempo Products lack of personnel planning also created problems, but for different reasons. There, personnel were hired to "take up the slack" when business was good. Once the crisis was over, the company found it had a number of people that it simply did not know what to do with.

Lack of Coordination. Another symptom of organizational growing pains is that many people are increasingly unaware of the exact nature of their jobs and how these jobs relate to those of others. This creates a situation in which people and departments do whatever they want to do and say that the remaining tasks are "not our responsibility." Constant bickering between people and departments over responsibilities may ensue. The organization may become a group of isolated and sometimes warring factions.

These problems typically result from the lack of an organization chart and precise role and responsibility definitions. Relationships between people and between departments as well as individual responsibilities may be unclear. As you will see in the cases of Metro Realty and Tempo Products, people can become frustrated by this ambiguity and begin creating their own definitions of their roles, which may not always be in the best interests of the firm. The president of Metro Realty vividly described this phenomenon when he said, "We were a collection of little offices working towards our goals without consideration for the good of the company."

The isolation of departments from one another may result in duplication of effort or in tasks that remain incomplete because they are "someone else's responsibility." Constant arguments between departments may also occur over territory and organizational resources. You have seen how this occurred at Custom Printing, and you will see in Chapter Six that Tempo Products also suffered from the effects of the need to define and protect territory.

Lack of Perceived Direction. Another typical growing pain is a widespread lack of understanding of where the firm is headed. Employees may complain that, "the company has no identity" and either blame upper management for not providing enough information about the company's future direction or, worse, believe that not even upper management knows what that direction will be. Basically, there has been a communication breakdown.

When insufficient communication is combined with rapid changes, as is often the case in growing firms, employees may begin to feel anxious. To relieve this anxiety, they may either create their own networks for obtaining the desired information or come to believe that they know the company's direction even though management has not actually communicated this information. Both these strategies were used by Tempo Products employees. Employees' speculations as well as "real" information obtained from people who were close to senior management circulated freely on the company's grapevine. Rumors were rampant, but in fact very few people really knew why certain changes were being made. Hence, employees experienced a significant amount of anxiety.

If anxiety increases to the point where it becomes unbearable, employees may begin leaving the firm. As we described in the Introduction, this happened at Custom Printing.

Insufficient Number of Good Managers. Although a firm may have a significant number of people who hold the title of "manager," it may not have many good managers. Managers may complain that they have responsibility, but no authority. Employees may complain about the lack of direction or feedback that their managers provide. The organization may notice that some of its components have significantly higher or lower productivity than others. It may also be plagued by managers who constantly complain that they do not have time to complete their administrative responsibilities because they are too busy increasing business. When any or all of these events occur, something is wrong with the management function of the organization.

As was the case at Custom Printing, the problem may be that the company has promoted successful "doers" (salespeople, office workers, and so on) to the role of manager, assuming that they will also be successful in this role. These two roles require significantly different skills, however. Thus, without proper training, many "doers" will fail in the manager's role. Their tendency to continue "doing" will show itself in poor delegation skills and poor coordination of the activities of others. Subordinates may complain that they do not know what they are supposed to do.

Problems like these suggest that the company is not devoting sufficient resources to developing a pool of managerial talent. It may be relying too much on on-the-job training rather than on formal management development programs.

Management problems may also result from real or perceived organizational constraints that restrict a manager's authority. In the case of Tempo Products, you will see how the perception that only top management could make decisions greatly affected lower-level managers' effectiveness. One person at this firm described the managers as "people with no real responsibility." The feeling that only upper management has decision-making responsibility is common in firms making the transition to professional management. It is a relic from the days when the founding entrepreneur made all the firm's decisions.

Desire to Do Everything Oneself. Increasingly, as people become frustrated by the difficulty of getting things done in an organization, they come to feel that "if I want to get something done correctly, I have to do it myself." This symptom, like lack of coordination, is caused by a lack of clearly defined roles, responsibilities, and linkages between roles.

As was discussed previously, when roles and responsibilities are not clearly defined, individuals or departments tend to act on their own because they do not know whose responsibility a given task is. They may also do the task themselves to avoid confrontation, since the person or department to whom they are trying to delegate a responsibility may refuse it.

Operating under this philosophy, departments become isolated from one another, and teamwork becomes minimal. Each part of the company "does its own thing" without considering the good of the whole. Communication between management and lower levels of the organization and between departments may be minimal because the organization has no formal system through which information can be channeled. You will see how the lack of coordination between areas can lead to productivity problems and inefficiencies when you read the Metro Realty and Tempo Products cases.

Feeling That Meetings Are a Waste of Time. Recognizing that there is a need for better coordination and communication, the growing organization may begin to hold meetings. Unfortunately, at many firms these meetings are nothing more than discussions between people. They have no planned agendas, and often they have no designated leader. As a consequence, the meetings become a free-for-all, tend to drag on interminably, and seldom result in decisions. People feel frustrated and conclude that "our meetings are a waste of time."

Other complaints about meetings involve lack of follow-up on decisions that are made. Some companies schedule yearly or monthly planning meetings during which goals are set for individual employees, departments, and the company as a whole. These sessions are a waste of time if people ignore the goals that have been set or fail to monitor their progress towards these goals. As you will see, Metro Realty's budgeting process suffered from this condition. In a frustrating "yearly exercise," managers met and set goals, then met again the following year with no idea of whether they had achieved the previous year's goals.

A further example of ineffective use of meeting time may appear in the performance appraisal process. In many organizations that are beginning to make the transition to professional management, performance appraisals are merely discussions between supervisor and subordinate. Objective performance goals may not be set or, if set, may not be monitored by employee or manager. Managers in these firms also tend to avoid providing negative feedback. Without such feedback, employees cannot learn what they need to do to improve performance. Because little real information is exchanged, performance appraisal meetings are a waste of both supervisor's and subordinate's time. In Chapters Five and Six you will see how Metro Realty and Tempo Products suffered from ineffective performance appraisals.

Lack of Follow-Up. Another sign of an entrepreneurship with growing pains is a lack of follow-up after plans are made. Recognizing that the need for planning is greater than in the past, an entrepreneur may introduce a planning process. People go through the motions of preparing business plans, but the things that were planned just do not get done.

In some cases there is no follow-up because the company has not yet developed systems adequate to monitor its goals. For example, many firms desire to monitor financial goals but have not developed an accounting system that can provide the information needed to do so. Metro Realty suffered from this deficiency.

In other cases, follow-up does not occur because personnel have not received proper training in setting, monitoring, and evaluating goals. They set goals that cannot be achieved or cannot be measured, or they do not know how to evaluate and provide useful feedback on goal achievement. These problems tend to appear most often in the performance appraisal process. You will read more about them in Chapters Five and Six.

Feelings of Insecurity. As a consequence of other organizational growing pains, employees begin to feel insecure about their places in the firm. Typically, the entrepreneur has become anxious about problems facing the organization and has therefore hired a "heavyweight" manager from outside. This action may have been accompanied by the termination of one or more current managers. Employees feel anxious partly because they do not understand the reasons for these and other changes. When anxiety becomes too high, it may result in morale problems or excessive turnover.

Employees may also become insecure because they are unable to see the value of their position to the firm. This occurs when roles and responsibilities are not clearly defined and terminations are also occurring. Employees begin to wonder whether they will be the next to "get the axe." In an attempt to protect themselves, they keep their activities secret and do not "make waves." This results in isolation and a decrease in teamwork.

Entire departments may come to suffer from the need to remain isolated in order to protect themselves from being eliminated. This can lead to a certain amount of schizophrenia among employees. They begin to ask, "Am I loyal to my department or to the organization at large?" This happened at Tempo Products, as you will see in Chapter Six.

Sales Increase Without Profit Increase. If all the other growing pains are permitted to exist, one final symptom may emerge. In some instances, sales continue to increase while profits remain flat, so that the company is succeeding only in increasing its workload. In the worst cases, sales increase while overall profits actually decline. As you will see in the chapters that follow, companies may begin to lose money without having any idea why. The business loss can be quite significant, even though sales are up.

In a significant number of companies, the decline in profits may be the result of an underlying philosophy that stresses sales. People in such companies may say, "If sales are good, then profit will also be good," or "Profit will take care of itself." Profit in these companies is not an explicit goal but merely whatever remains after expenses.

In sales-oriented companies, people often become accustomed to spending whatever they need to in order to make a sale or promote the organization. For example, at Tempo Products, employees believed that it was important to the company's image to always "go first class." They made no effort to control costs, since they believed that no matter what they did, the organization would always be profitable. Organizations may also suffer because of systems that reward employees for achieving sales goals rather than profit goals. You will see examples of these problems in Chapters Five and Six.

Measuring Organizational Growing Pains

To assist the management of an entrepreneurial company in measuring the organization's growing pains, we have developed the questionnaire shown in Exhibit 1. This questionnaire presents ten organizational growing pains that have been identified in a wide variety of entrepreneurial companies with annual sales revenues ranging from less than $1 million to over $1 billion. Responses to the questionnaire are entered on a Likert-type five-point scale with descriptors ranging from "to a very great extent" to "to a very slight extent." By placing check marks in the appropriate columns, the respondent indicates the extent to which he or she feels each of the ten growing pains characterizes the company.

Scoring the Questionnaire. Once the questionnaire has been completed, the number of check marks in each column is totaled and recorded on line 11. Each item on line 11 is then multiplied by the corresponding weight on line 12, and the total is recorded on line 13. For example, Exhibit 1 shows four check marks in column B. Accordingly, we multiply 4 by the weight of 4 and record the result, 16, on line 13 of column B.

The next step is to determine the sum of the numbers on line 13. This total represents the organization's growing pains score. It can range from 10, which is the lowest possible or most favorable score, to 50 which is the highest possible or most unfavorable score.

Interpreting the Scores. Drawing on our research concerning the degree of seriousness of problems indicated by different growing pain scores, we have worked out the color-coding scheme shown in Table 4. More detailed interpretation of score ranges is as follows.

A green score represents a fairly healthy organization. It suggests that everything is probably functioning in a manner satisfactory for the organization at its current stage of development.

Exhibit 1. Organizational Growing Pains Questionnaire.

Growing Pain	A To a very great extent	B To a great extent	C To some extent	D To a slight extent	E To a very slight extent
1. People feel that there are not enough hours in the day.		x			
2. People spend too much time "putting out fires."		x			
3. Many people are not aware of what others are doing.	x				
4. People lack understanding of where the firm is heading.			x		
5. There are too few good managers.		x			
6. Everybody feels, "I have to do it myself if I want it to get done correctly."			x		
7. Most people feel our meetings are a waste of time.				x	
8. When plans are made, there is very little follow-up, and things just don't get done.		x			
9. Some people feel insecure about their place in the firm.				x	
10. The firm has continued to grow in sales but not in profits.	x				

SCORING

	A	B	C	D	E
11. Add the total number of responses in each column.	2	4	2	2	0
12. Multiply the number on line 11 by the number on line 12 and record the result on line 13.	5	4	3	2	1
13. Result of line 11 times line 12.	10	16	6	4	0
14. Add the numbers on line 13 in columns A-E and place the result on this line.	36				

Table 4. Interpretation of Organizational Growing Pains
Questionnaire Scores.

Score Range	Color	Interpretation
1. 10–14	Green	Everything OK
2. 15–19	Yellow	Some things to watch
3. 20–29	Orange	Some areas that need attention
4. 30–39	Red	Some very significant problems
5. 40–50	Purple	A potentially dangerous situation

A yellow score indicates that the organization is basically healthy, but there are some areas of concern. It is like hearing from your doctor, "Your cholesterol is in the normal range but on the high side. It's something to watch and be careful about but not an immediate concern."

An orange score indicates that some organizational problems require attention. They may not be too serious yet, but corrective action should be taken before they become so.

A red score is a clear warning of present or impending problems. Immediate corrective action is required.

A purple score indicates a dangerous, perhaps deadly situation. The organization is in distress and may be on the verge of collapse. There may not be enough time to save it.

If a firm's score exceeds 20, a more in-depth analysis to identify problems and develop recommendations for future action is probably required. Such a score may be a signal that the firm has reached a new stage in its development and must make major, qualitative changes. Failure to pay attention to a score of this magnitude can produce very painful results. For example, the questionnaire shown in Exhibit 1 was completed by Joe McBride, who was the CEO of Custom Printing, the firm we described in the Introduction to this book. Custom Printing's score, based on Joe's perceptions, was 36. This "red" score tallies well with the fact that, as you saw, Custom Printing was in serious trouble.

Average Scores for Different Business Sizes and Industries. Table 5 presents average organizational growing pains scores of companies with different annual revenues based on our extensive research. As can be seen, companies of every size experience some growing pains. As organizations grow, growing pains tend to increase until companies reach a significantly large size. Our data suggest that the most significant problems begin to be experienced when a company's annual revenues reach $10 million (stage II to stage III organizations) and continue until revenues exceed $1 billion.

Table 6 shows scores broken down by type of industry. Clearly, timing of the occurrence of significant organizational growing pains differs across industries.

In the service industry, a time of concern seems to occur in the $25 to $499 million revenue range, and a potential danger point arises in the $500 million to $1 billion range. The data suggest that it is very difficult to manage a large service company. Service companies in the $10 to $24 million range seem to have the fewest growing pains.

High-technology companies do not appear to experience significant problems until they reach the $25 to $99 million range of revenues. Problems then arise and continue into the $100 million to $499 million range. Low-technology companies, in contrast, experience significant problems beginning at the $5 to $9 million revenue range, but they appear to resolve their problems by the time they reach $25 million in revenues.

We have the most complete information on the pattern of growing pains experienced by financial companies. As can be seen in Table 6, this industry has a pattern of growing pains consistent with the overall pattern. Its growing pains increase until revenues exceed $24 million. They then drop, but they begin rising again when revenues reach $100 million. Above $1 billion they show a second drop.

The information presented here suggests that entrepreneurs in different industries need to be concerned with growing pains at different periods of their organizations' lives. For those in the service, low-tech, and finance industries, a critical period occurs at the $10 to $24 million revenue range. For high-tech industries, this critical point occurs when revenues begin to exceed $25 million. These data also indicate that large ($500 million to $1 billion in

Table 5. Organizational Growing Pains by Company Size.

Size (Revenues)	Average Growing Pains Score
Less than $1 million (stage I)	26.00 (orange)
$1–9 million (stage II)	28.00 (orange)
$10–99 million (stage III)	31.00 (red)
$100–499 million (stage IV)	34.00 (red)
$500 million–$1 billion	38.00 (red)
More than $1 billion	25.00 (orange)

Table 6. Organizational Growing Pains in Different Industries.

Size (Revenues)	Overall	Service	High-tech	Low-tech	Finance
Less than $1 million (stage I)	26.48 Orange	27.57 Orange	26.12 Orange	24.43 Orange	23.00 Orange
$1–4 million (stage II)	27.77 Orange	28.16 Orange	27.25 Orange	27.88 Orange	27.79 Orange
$5–9 million (stage II)	29.22 Orange	28.19 Orange	29.58 Orange	31.44 Red	28.80 Orange
$10–24 million (stage III)	31.26 Red	25.33 Orange	29.75 Orange	32.60 Red	31.82 Red
$25–99 million (stage III)	29.20 Orange	31.27 Red	30.88 Red	24.50 Orange	30.29 Red
$100–499 million (stage IV)	34.45 Red	34.50 Red	35.50 Red		33.67 Red
$500 million –$1 billion	38.50 Red	40.00 Purple			37.00 Red
More than $1 billion	25.00 Orange				25.00 Orange

revenues) service industries experience the most severe organizational growing pains.

While the data presented in Table 6 indicate that there are certain stages of growth in which organizational growing pains are likely to be severe, these growing pains at any stage can be alleviated. This is best done through early detection of problems and careful plans for handling them.

Summary

This chapter has presented an in-depth discussion of the most common organizational growing pains. These are characterized by the statements (1) "There are not enough hours in the day," (2) "We are always 'putting out fires,' " (3) "Coordination between people and departments is lacking," (4) "People cannot perceive the company's direction," (5) "There are too few good managers," (6) "People feel that they must do everything themselves," (7) "People feel that meetings are a waste of time," (8) "Plans are not followed up," (9) "People feel insecure about their place in the company," and (10) "Sales are increasing, but profit isn't."

The chapter has also presented a method for assessing the extent to which a company suffers from these growing pains. The company's score on the Organizational Growing Pains Questionnaire can suggest both the extent of its problems and specific needs for action.

Finally, the chapter has provided information on the degree of organizational growing pains experienced by companies of different sizes and in different types of businesses. Variations exist here, but it is clear that organizations of all sizes and types experience some growing pains. Managers of rapidly growing companies of any size or type must learn to recognize organizational growing pains and take steps to alleviate them so that their organizations can continue to operate successfully.

PART II

⚭⚭⚭⚭

Management Strategies
for Each Stage
of Organizational Growth

Part One of this book presented a framework for understanding the development of successful organizations. It explained the six key areas or tasks that make up the pyramid of organizational development. It also identified and examined the four stages of growth of organizations. It presented the four major steps involved in making the transition from one stage of growth to the next. Finally, it described the organizational growing pains that result when a firm has not been fully successful in its development and presented a way to measure and interpret them.

Part Two will examine the issues involved in developing successful organizations at each stage of growth. It will also study the nature of the transitions that must be made in moving from stage I to stages II, III, and IV. It will draw on a variety of case studies of organizations at different stages of growth.

Chapter Four begins by discussing the steps involved in developing a successful stage I company. It gives several illustrations of firms that have been successful in accomplishing this stage of development and examines the problems faced by each company. Examples cited range from Domino's Pizza and Mrs. Fields' Cookies to Liz Claiborne, Apple Computer, and Ashton-Tate.

Chapter Four also examines the process and problems involved in developing successful stage II organizations. It describes some growing pains that may result when the process of organizational development has not been fully successful, especially when a firm has not developed the operational systems it needs to function well at stage II.

Chapter Five examines the case of a company that made the transition from stage II to stage III. It describes the company's situation, the nature of its growing pains, and the actions it took to make a successful transition between these stages. This case study also illustrates the most common problems involved in making the transition from entrepreneurship to professional management, especially in developing management systems.

Chapter Six examines a firm that is making the transition from stage III to stage IV. It discusses the issues involved in developing an explicit corporate culture.

4

The New Venture
and Expansion Stages

This chapter deals with the issues involved in developing successful entrepreneurial organizations at stages I and II of organizational growth. It examines the tasks that must be performed to establish a successful new venture (stage I) and deals with the typical growing pains that arise during the expansion that takes place after a company has been successfully established (stage II).

Developing Successful Stage I Organizations

In the first stage of an organization's development or life cycle, the company is a new venture. This stage embraces the period from an organization's birth to the point at which it begins to experience rapid growth (usually at about $1 million in annual revenues). The first section of this chapter identifies the key problems or challenges involved in building a successful new venture and provides several illustrations of actual firms that have successfully met these challenges. It examines why these firms have been successful.

The Key Issues at Stage I. The key challenges or problems to be solved in developing a successful new venture are identifying a market need and finding a way to satisfy that need by providing a product or service. The skills required to solve these problems are essentially the classic entrepreneurial skills: the ability to see a market need, the willingness to make a risky investment to create a business that attempts to satisfy that need, and the ability to create an embryonic organization that is capable of providing the required products or services.

The primary basis of entrepreneurship is an idea. The idea may be the product of long, tedious planning and research or of a brilliant, almost accidental, insight.

Hot Rock, Inc.: A Classic Entrepreneurial Success. To understand the process of developing a successful stage I organization, let us review an actual example of a recent entrepreneurial success. In February, 1983, two Harvard Business School students sipping coffee at Boston's Logan Airport casually began to discuss an idea for promoting record sales.* They wondered: What if ordering a record could be as easy as making a phone call? What if someone sitting in a living room could simply pick up the telephone and order a new album that he or she had just heard? One year later, the two student entrepreneurs had converted this concept into a successful business called Hot Rock, Inc. How did that happen?

The basis for the pair's ultimate success was a perceived market need. The two entrepreneurs, Michael Wigley and Jerry De La Vega, together with a third colleague, David Ishag, saw a potential solution to a problem that plagued the record industry: As the buyers of records grew older and became increasingly affluent, they had less time to shop. As a result, record companies became less likely to reach this segment of the market through the traditional channels of distribution. The entrepreneurs were also aware of the tremendous popularity of MTV and believed that it drew a broader audience than the eighteen to thirty-four age group that was the core market of record companies.

The basic concept of this new venture was elegant in its simplicity. By combining the convenience of telephone sales, the advertising penetration of MTV, and the market's demand for rock, the entrepreneurs identified a market niche that was not being satisfied. They put together a prospectus, raised $120,000 in venture capital, and began their firm. The target market was viewers of

* Michael B. Abelson, "Students Turn Hot Idea into Successful Firm," *Los Angeles Times,* May 8, 1984, sec. 4.

MTV, who were provided with Hot Rock's toll-free telephone number twenty-four hours a day.

After just a few months of operation, the firm projected sales of $6.7 million for its first year. It had successfully solved the critical problems of a stage I organization: identification of a market and development of a product or service relevant to that market's need. Although the fledgling firm will undoubtedly face other challenges, it represents a classic example of new venture success and illustrates the entrepreneurial skills required for such success.

Other Examples of New Venture Success. There are many other examples of entrepreneurial success. Let us examine some of them to develop further insights into the process and skills required to develop a successful stage I company.

There have been a number of entrepreneurial successes in the computer industry, especially in microcomputers. One of the most spectacular success stores is that of Apple Computer. Apple was founded by Steven Jobs and Steven Wozniak. It was based on the perceived market for a "personal" computer: a small, relatively inexpensive computer that was "user friendly." Following this concept, the firm grew from being housed in a garage to having more than $1 billion in sales in 1983.

Adam Osborne, who founded Osborne Computer Corporation, had the concept of a relatively low-priced, easy-to-use computer that was also portable. His idea was a spin-off of the personal computer concept pioneered by Apple Computer but Osborne identified a new market niche when he made his computers easy to carry. For a few years, Osborne Computer was one of the fastest-growing companies in business history. In 1981, the firm's first full year of operation, its sales were $5.8 million. By 1982, sales had grown to $68.8 million.

William Zimmerman founded Pic 'N' Save with the idea that the firm could buy manufacturers' excess inventory cheaply and sell it at large discounts to customers. The firm's merchandise constantly changes, as it shops the world for surplus goods. The company had grown to more than $235 million in annual revenues by 1984.

Another recent example of entrepreneurial success is Ashton-Tate. The firm's major product is dBASE II, a software package. Ashton-Tate was founded by Hal Lashley and George Tate. The firm took the name of George Tate and "Ashton," a large blue-and-yellow parrot. Ashton lives in his cage in the firm's offices in California.

Ashton-Tate's history is a vintage example of entrepreneurship. Initially, Lashley and Tate founded a part-time software distribution business. They then came across a software product developed by a third party and made an agreement to distribute it. They named the product dBASE II. The product was an extraordinary success because it filled a market need and was marketed well.

Although many of the examples just cited are in the computer industry, high technology is not a prerequisite for entrepreneurial success. Federal Express is an example of a company based on a service rather than a product, and a relatively unsophisticated service at that.

Frederick W. Smith was the architect of Federal Express. At the time the company was founded, Emery Air Freight dominated the package delivery business. Emery had built a successful business on the assumption that the major cost in air freight involved weight and, therefore, air carrier charges. This notion made sense for heavy items but not for small packages or letters. Federal Express built a different system, geared to the goal of minimizing handling costs rather than air carrier costs. It focused on a different niche—small packages.

The success of both Debbie Fields of Mrs. Fields' Cookies and David Liederman of David's Cookies not only shows that a successful new venture can be developed from a very old, familiar product; it also shows that more than one niche can be filled successfully within the same market. Both entrepreneurs created successful new ventures by developing stores to make and market over-the-counter chocolate chip cookies.

David's Cookies defined a market for consumers who prefer large chunks of chocolate in a thin, buttery cookie that is not sold until it cools. Mrs. Fields' Cookies, in contrast, defined a market for a more traditional chocolate chip cookie, with smaller chips in a larger-sized cookie that is served warm. Both firms have been quite successful.

Mitchell Kapor worked as a disc jockey, studied to be a Transcendental Meditation instructor, and became a mental health counselor. In 1979, he bought an Apple computer. He wrote two programs, called VisiPlot and VisiTrend, that simplified business graphs and charts. He then took the profits from these products, together with venture capital, and founded Lotus Development Corporation in April 1982. The firm produced the very successful program called Lotus 1-2-3. When the firm went public in October 1983, Kapor's stock was worth more than $80 million.

During its first year of business, 1983, Compaq Computer Corporation's sales zoomed to $111.2 million. The firm's product was a portable version of the IBM personal computer. It was compatible with the IBM PC and sold at a lower price.

In 1960, Thomas S. Monaghan and his brother borrowed $500 to open a small restaurant in Ypsilanti, Michigan, a small suburb near Detroit. Its name was Dominik's Pizza. Today, the firm is called Domino's Pizza and has more than 800 stores, 6,000 employees, and annual sales revenues in excess of $260 million.

Monaghan originally went into the pizza parlor business because he liked to eat pizzas. He and his brother knew very little about the restaurant business. The firm was undercapitalized; as Monaghan explains, "I think I had $77 in my checkbook."* His original goal was to operate a pizzeria in order to generate enough funds to pay his way through architecture school. However, he soon found himself working more than 100 hours a week.

Monaghan's basic concept was to sell a pizza at a price lower than that charged by any of his competitors and to provide free delivery. The concept was an immediate success, and Monaghan found himself so busy that he did not have time to sit down and pay the bills.

The firm had five sizes of pizza, from six to sixteen inches. There was an enormous demand for six-inch pizzas, but they were unprofitable for the firm because of the labor and delivery costs.

*"Starting Small and Growing Big: The Essentials of Managing Growth," *Dividend*, Winter 1983, p. 8.

One day, Monaghan stopped the sale of the six-inch pizza. Suddenly, instead of losing four or five hundred dollars a week, he found himself making the same amount. As he put it, "I was rich!"

The keys to Domino's success were, first, the ability of its founder to identify a market niche and, second, his ability to build a business to satisfy it. Monaghan's concept was the simple notion of delivery of pizzas. This may not seem like a brilliant or unique strategy today, but it was a novel idea when Monaghan pioneered it. Monaghan states, "Basically, any place that delivered, you really wouldn't want to buy a pizza from, because if they had a good product they wouldn't have to deliver. Nobody delivered unless they were crazy or stupid, and I was both." Indeed, nobody wanted delivery except customers—so Monaghan focused on delivery as his competitive advantage. This led to his market niche, the place within the overall market where he had a strong foothold.

The basic idea behind the success of Liz Claiborne, Inc., was also simple. The concept was to develop lines of fashionable, well-made sportswear that could be worn to the office. To keep distribution costs low, the firm focused on department stores, thereby minimizing the need for a sales force. The Claiborne concept was successful, and the rest is history.

Keys to a Successful Stage I Firm

New ventures in computers, clothing, and cookies, not to mention package delivery, pizza, and rock records, would not seem to have much in common. Yet if we look closely, we will see that each of these diverse businesses demonstrated certain fundamental abilities. Possession of these abilities is the prerequisite for developing a successful new venture.

1. The ability to define a market need;
2. The ability to develop, acquire, or provide a product or service that will satisfy the identified market need; and
3. The ability to build an organization that is capable of functioning on a day-to-day basis to provide the product or service.

Let us discuss each of these critical factors further.

Ability to Define a Market Need. The most fundamental prerequisite for success as a new venture is the ability to identify and define a market need that is not currently being satisfied or that can be satisfied in a different way (higher quality, lower cost, and so on). Each of the firms we described was able to do this.

Apple Computer saw the need for a personal computer that the average person, not just the computer "hacker," could use. The company is following the same strategy today with its Macintosh, which it advertises as the computer "for the rest of us." Adam Osborne perceived the need for a portable computer, and Compaq saw the need for a relatively inexpensive, IBM-compatible portable computer. Mitchell Kapor saw the need for certain computer software. David Liederman and Debbie Fields saw an unsatisfied need for "gourmet" chocolate chip cookies. Tom Monaghan saw the need for home delivery of good pizza. The two Harvard Business School students saw an opportunity to satisfy the need for convenient purchasing of rock records. Fred Smith saw the need for inexpensive, rapid delivery of small packages. Liz Claiborne saw the need for medium-priced fashionable clothing that could be worn to work.

It should be noted that the needs these entrepreneurs saw were not necessarily for a new product, although some of the products were new. Others, such as Mrs. Fields' and David's Cookies, were merely reconceptualizations of existing products or services.

Ability to Develop a Relevant Product or Service. The second major task in developing a successful stage I firm is providing a product or service that satisfies the market need the company has identified. Apple Computer was not the first firm to perceive the need for a personal computer, but it was the first to develop an acceptable product and market it successfully.

Some entrepreneurs do not succeed in developing successful new ventures because, while they are able to see the market for a product, they are not able to develop the required product or service.

Ability to Develop an Organization to Provide the Product or Service. The third requirement for a successful stage I company is the ability to develop an organization capable of providing the chosen product or service to customers. This involves developing the basic systems for day-to-day operation of the firm as well as finding the people needed to staff the organization.

If the three things just described are done well, a company will pass the first test of survival. It may then begin to grow rapidly, and this growth will create a new set of problems to be solved. These new problems are the subject of the next section of this chapter, which deals with the development of successful stage II companies.

Developing Successful Stage II Organizations

The second stage of organizational development is the rapid growth stage. This stage begins after a firm has solved the three critical problems involved in establishing a new venture. It may start very quickly or only after many years.

Hot Rock, Inc.: Growing Pains. Hot Rock, Inc., whose success in the new venture stage we described in the previous section, had hardly got started when it began to experience rapid growth. According to Michael Wigley: "We thought that our promos would generate between twenty-four and twenty-five calls a day, based upon our system's capacity and the demographics of our ads. As it turned out, we generated a lot more calls than expected."* By the firm's seventeenth day in business, it had already received 50,000 inquiries.

The firm grew at a rate of 19 percent a week for the first few months. At this rate of growth, it was not surprising that the firm overran its organizational resources, systems, and capabilities. Demand exceeded the firm's telephone capacity and computer capability twice over, and demand for cash forced the firm to sell an additional 39 percent of its holdings. The entrepreneurs found themselves working eighteen to twenty hours a day.

In brief, although Hot Rock was only a few months old, it had already begun to experience organizational growing pains that warned of a need to make the transition from a stage I to a stage II firm. It found that its resources (people, cash, inventory, telephone equipment, and computers) were insufficient to handle

* Abelson, "Students," p. 2.

the volume of business it had generated, and its day-to-day operational systems were inadequate to support the volume of current and anticipated future business.

The name of the game had changed. The critical tasks facing the firm were no longer to identify a market and product or to provide more and more of the product; rather, they were to acquire the resources and develop the operational systems needed to facilitate anticipated future growth. Hot Rock, Inc., is currently in the process of making the required transition. Only the future will tell whether it will do so successfully.

Unfortunately, many firms that successfully meet the challenges of growth stage I ultimately flounder in stage II. This happens because the problems of managing a rapidly growing organization are in many ways fundamentally different from those of setting up a new venture. A stage II firm requires capabilities different from those of a stage I firm, and the managers of such an organization require different skills. Not all organizations and all entrepreneurs, even those who were brilliant in stage I, can handle the required metamorphosis.

The "Osborne Syndrome." One of the most spectacular and tragic examples of a firm that failed to make the transition from stage I to stage II is Osborne Computer Corporation. Because Osborne's experience is such a classic example, we call the phenomenon it exemplifies the "Osborne syndrome." This is the phenomenon in which an organization that has experienced rapid success as an entrepreneurial venture soon experiences equally rapid decline because it has failed to make the transition from an entrepreneurship to a professionally managed firm. As Adam Osborne himself has stated: "When you become an entrepreneur you can go up awfully fast, but you can go down just as fast. It's so ephemeral, like actors who end up committing suicide. One day they're famous, the next nobody knows who the hell they are."*

Osborne Computer Corporation began when Adam Osborne recognized the market for a portable microcomputer. Despite skepticism, Osborne produced and marketed his machines and, in

*Robert A. Mamis, "'Face to Face' with Adam Osborne," *Inc.*, November 1983, p. 21.

doing so, created a new market. The firm experienced extraordinarily rapid growth, soon achieving more than $100 million in annual revenues and employing more than 1,000 people.

Osborne's success was the classic entrepreneur's dream come true; but it turned into the classic entrepreneurial nightmare when the firm experienced its now-well-publicized difficulties. When some suppliers sued to collect $4.5 million, Osborne filed for bankruptcy under Chapter XI of the Federal Bankruptcy Code.

What caused the fall of Osborne Computer Corporation after its meteoric rise? Although the answer to this question is complex, a key to the basic problem was stated by Adam Osborne himself in reflecting on what had happened to his firm. As he said, the firm "had existed only eighteen months in terms of operation—hardly time to get my feet wet; all of a sudden the job was a whole different order of magnitude. I realized it was no longer an entrepreneurial operation in any conceivable way."* In spite of this recognition, Osborne was unable to make the required changes in himself or his company.

Unfortunately, there is a pattern in what happened to Adam Osborne. Unless entrepreneurs learn from this story, they may someday find themselves experiencing the "Osborne syndrome."

After the initial success of a new entrepreneurial venture, a rapidly growing firm will inevitably experience the kind of organizational growing pains we described in Chapter Three, just as Osborne Computer Corporation did. As we have stated, these pains are normal, but they are a warning, symptoms of a disease that can be fatal if left untreated. The "fatality" is the Osborne syndrome we have just described. The key to avoiding the Osborne syndrome is recognizing the warning inherent in an organization's growing pains and dealing with these symptoms before the condition becomes terminal.

Other Examples of Problems at Stage II. Let us now look at several other companies that experienced organizational growing pains strong enough to put them in danger of suffering the Osborne syndrome.

* Mamis, "Face to Face," p. 22.

An industrial products distributor had grown from $3 million in annual sales to $15 million, but profits had not increased proportionately. Indeed, they had actually begun to decline. The firm's accounting information could not pinpoint the reasons for these profitability problems. Inventory had accumulated in the warehouse, but no one could say how much of each item there was or where it was located, since the firm's inventory control system was manual and not kept up to date. The firm hired an ever-increasing number of people to cope with day-to-day operational pressures, but many of these people worked without supervision because their managers were too busy "putting out fires." The sales staff included some outstanding people, but others were simply nonproductive. The firm was beginning to lose accounts because of a series of embarrassing foul-ups such as missed delivery dates, incorrect merchandise shipments, and erroneous billings.

A successful $35 million soft goods manufacturer that had grown rapidly suddenly found itself constantly struggling to "put out fires." Employees were unaware of what other employees were doing. The firm had the obvious goals of manufacturing and selling merchandise, but it had no concept of what it wanted to become. The firm did not have a profit plan or departmental budgets; it could determine profitability only at the end of the fiscal year, after the opportunity to correct problems had passed. It had no performance appraisal system, so people tended to do whatever they wanted to do. As long as the firm continued to grow in sales, these problems were "merely inefficiencies." When the economy suddenly turned sour, however, these growing pains almost became terminal, and the firm's venture capital group had the company's president replaced.

A $75 million manufacturer began to experience high turnover and low morale, with people complaining, "If I want to get anything done around here, I have to do it myself." The firm had no plans, no goals, no formal organizational structure, no accountability, an almost incredible number of people running around doing things without direction, and a dizzying array of operational problems. No one seemed to know who should report to whom. The firm was still profitable because it had identified a market niche, but it had spawned competitors during the last few years, some of them people who had left the original firm. These competitors were now growing rapidly and seemed about to pass the original firm in size and profits.

A $100 million firm found that parts of the organization were making decisions affecting other parts without informing people, leading to costly inefficiencies and duplication of efforts. For example, materials delivered to a warehouse had to be returned to the vendor because of lack of space to store them. Fiefdoms had been built up at the senior executive level, and there was little communication except on a vertical basis. Since the firm was successful, people had got into the habit of "going first class" and operating with a "country club" mentality. Looming on the horizon, meanwhile, were some of the industry's bigger players, who had noticed the firm's success with its market niche and were planning their own entries.

A $150 million software manufacturer had had great success with a single product, growing from a garage-size operation to a significant firm. After about three years of good times, it found itself suddenly in trouble. Management development was so minimal that one department head said, "I was walked to the door of my department and told: 'Here is your department; manage it.' " The firm also experienced difficulty in developing new products to repeat its earlier success.

A $250 million industrial components distributor that had grown explosively found itself with extremely high personnel turnover. The firm was continuing to "push products out the door," but sales personnel were constantly infuriated to find that products they had sold and believed were in inventory could not be delivered because the firm's control system was hopelessly incorrect.

All the firms just described were initially successful organizations. They experienced various problems or growing pains because of differences in size and/or market conditions. They all have the potential for experiencing the Osborne syndrome: meteoric success followed by equally rapid failure.

Keys to a Successful Stage II Firm

All the firms we described in the last section experienced difficulties because of their failure to develop the increasingly complex operational systems that became necessary as they grew.

Osborne Computer required systems for control of inventories, cash management, and accounting information to facilitate the growth spurt that the company was experiencing. The industrial products distributor that had grown from $15 million to $43 million also had problems with its accounting and inventory management systems. The $35 million soft goods manufacturer lacked proper budgeting and performance appraisal systems and consequently found its staff "out of control." The $75 million manufacturer lacked both an adequate set of job descriptions and a set of overall plans or goals. The list could go on and on.

The basic problem all these companies faced was that the entrepreneurs who owned and managed them were more interested in the challenges presented at stage I than in those of stage II. Identification of a market and development of a product or service seem glamorous compared with the more mundane tasks involved in developing and refining the organizational plumbing or infrastructure. Unfortunately, while something like an accounting system may be unexciting, it is vital for a growing organization. The shipping dock may be a less elegant place than a well-appointed corporate headquarters, but if enough foul ups occur at the shipping dock, they can render the headquarters an expensive albatross.

If entrepreneurs want to make the successful transition from stage I to stage II, they must force themselves to be concerned about the organizational plumbing or operational systems required for day-to-day performance. Their survival depends on it.

Summary

This chapter has examined the development of successful stage I and stage II organizations. The keys to success at stage I are the ability to identify a market niche, provide a product or service appropriate to that niche, and develop the basic organization required to run the infant business.

If a firm is successful in stage I, it will begin to experience rapid growth. As a result, it is likely to develop a variety of organizational growing pains. These growing pains are normal, but they must not be ignored. They are the signal that it is time to begin the transition from an entrepreneurial to a professionally managed firm. Failure to successfully make this transition can lead to severe problems and, ultimately, to the Osborne syndrome (meteoric success followed by meteoric failure).

In the next chapter we will describe the problems and challenges involved in developing a professionally managed firm at stage III. We will present a case study of a firm called Metro Realty and show how it made the transition from stage II to stage III successfully.

5

The Professionalizing
Stage: Developing
Management Systems

During the entrepreneurial stages of growth (stages I and II), planning, control, and management development are done on an *ad hoc* basis in many firms, and a formal organization structure is practically nonexistent. Individuals and departments operate on a day-to-day basis, making adjustments in various systems to meet the demands of the environment in which the company operates. This may actually contribute to the success of entrepreneurial firms, but it can be quite detrimental once an organization reaches stage III.

As organizational growing pains resulting from the rapid growth that characterizes stage II increase in severity, senior management begins to realize (or should realize) that a qualitative change in the nature of their firm is needed. The firm has reached the threshold of stage III and must develop and formalize the management systems that are needed in a professionally managed firm.

As described in Chapter One, these management systems include planning, organization structure, management development and control. The systems help the company coordinate the functions of its personnel and departments, provide direction to its employees, and motivate employees to achieve organizational goals. Basically, management systems formalize many of the activities that

79

earlier, when the organization was small and growing, were performed through face-to-face interaction with personal leadership by the entrepreneur.

This chapter illustrates the process of making the transition from an entrepreneurship (stage I or stage II) to a professionally managed firm (stage III). It provides an example of the problems experienced by a rapidly growing company and the kinds of programs that can help an organization formalize its management systems and overcome its growing pains.

The chapter will focus on a case study of Metro Realty, an organization that was successful in transforming itself from an entrepreneurship to a professionally managed firm. We will describe the company's history; the growing pains it experienced as it rapidly increased in size, personnel, and revenues; and the program its management designed to help the company overcome its problems and make the transition to a stage III firm. In the concluding section of this chapter, we will discuss the implications of Metro Realty's experience for other companies who find themselves on the verge of this transformation.

The company described actually exists, although its name has been changed, and certain facts about its situation have been slightly modified in order to preserve its confidentiality. The basic situation described here really occurred in this company.

Metro Realty: Background

Harvey and Dolores Brown opened the first office of Metro Realty on July 5, 1938, in Center City, the heart of the metropolitan area. The company prospered and grew as a result of both the personal creativeness and dedication of the founders and their ability to recruit people who could contribute to the success of the firm. In 1963 Harvey Brown died, and a group of seven investors acquired Metro Realty. The company was, at this time, still a small entrepreneurial enterprise emphasizing residential real estate. It had three offices and thirty employees.

By 1970, little had changed since the company's founding. Metro Realty remained small in terms of employees, office space, and revenue and operated under a "family-style" management system. Its staff still consisted of twenty-eight to thirty people occupying three offices. The president of the company, Bob Mitchell, was expected to supervise the entire company's functioning, much as Harvey Brown had done from the company's inception until his death.

Metro still operated very effectively as an entrepreneurial firm as evidenced by its growth. Between 1970 and 1978, the total number of branch offices grew from three to eleven, and the total number of employees increased from 30 to 250. Revenues increased from $1 million to nearly $10 million in this same period. According to management, this prosperity resulted from the firm's ability to do certain things very well. These included knowing how to select locations, how to time moves, and how to recruit and train salespeople.

Growing Pains

Between 1970 and 1978, then, Metro Realty grew very rapidly in terms of sales, size, and personnel—and it was continuing to grow. By 1978, Metro included a management and leasing department, a loan and investment department, a referral department, an administrative department, and eleven branch sales offices, all seemingly operating successfully. Plans were even being made to acquire another realty firm, which would increase the company's size to twenty offices and about 500 employees.

Unfortunately, the organization's original structure could no longer support the enterprise that Metro had become. Everyone from the president to the sales associates could feel the impact of the problems that the company's rapid growth was creating. As one branch manager put it, "The attitude that now exists is that the company wants to be larger than it is and is moving faster in this direction than can be accommodated by its structure, leadership, and personnel." Lack of coordination in functions and activities was leading to increasing frustration among employees. Certain aspects of the company needed to be changed if it was to continue to be successful.

Culture. According to the president of Metro, "Part of the real estate culture is to tolerate poor performers," and Metro was no exception. At Metro, poor performers were tolerated partly because the culture emphasized being "part of a family," and one could not very easily dismiss a family member. Managers also retained poor performers in order to avoid conflict. The culture promoted the notion that it was better to keep such people than to disrupt the system by dismissing them.

A third factor that contributed to the problem of poor performance was the concept of productivity promoted at Metro. "Productivity" was considered to include anything from sending out flyers and making phone calls to actually completing a sale. Only the last-named activity directly contributed to the firm's revenues, but all three activities were regarded as "productive" in and of themselves. One cultural belief of the firm seemed to be, "If a person looks busy, he or she is productive." With an increased number of personnel, this loose definition of productivity was becoming quite costly.

A final component of the firm's culture that may have contributed to retaining poor performers was an apparent lack of concern with the costs related to retaining these individuals. Traditionally, Metro had been concerned only with revenue production. Profit was not an explicit goal; it was simply the amount of money that remained after commissions and other costs had been paid. Cost control, therefore, was not an important consideration, since the company was not explicitly concerned with retaining income for future use. As the firm grew, however, a critical need arose to change the culture toward one that emphasized profit and considered both costs and revenues. This new culture would not be able to tolerate poor performers.

Roles and Responsibilities. The roles and responsibilities of different management positions had not been clearly defined at Metro. The organization functioned on an *ad hoc* basis, with responsibilities often overlapping. This lack of role definitions had not detracted from the functioning of the entrepreneurial firm, but it became a source of frustration as the company expanded. One manager, perhaps speaking for many, said that he was "fed up with the role confusion."

The ambiguity of role definitions also contributed to an unwillingness to accept responsibility. At Metro, it was relatively easy for managers to blame problems on other people or levels in the organization. There was no way to hold specific managers responsible for specific tasks, since responsibilities had not been clearly defined.

Planning. Like many activities, corporate planning at Metro was done on an *ad hoc* basis. Metro had never had a written plan that outlined the financial and nonfinancial goals, objectives, and targets of the organization, and the size and success of the company had led its members to believe that such an effort was not warranted. As the organization grew, however, the need to plan for the company's future became apparent. The personnel at Metro began to desire some direction to guide their actions. It seemed that the company could no longer function effectively without goals.

Budgets and Accounting System. An important component of a company's planning process is a yearly budget that states financial goals. Unfortunately, the administrative systems necessary to help Metro know how it was performing financially and plan for its future were not formalized.

The budgeting process at Metro had traditionally been only a yearly "exercise," since managers had no system by which to monitor costs and revenue. They received little feedback from the organization concerning the amount they had spent or the profit they had earned. Most of the available financial statements provided information only on the performance of the organization as a whole, not on that of individual branch offices. The small amount of information on branch office performance that was available was often incomplete and/or inaccurate. Further, one branch manager suggested that he didn't believe the accounting information that was being provided to him; he said he "couldn't understand where the numbers were coming from."

Metro clearly needed a more formalized budgeting process, but its underdeveloped accounting system did not support such an effort. Metro's system of accounting was described by an independent accounting firm as having "no thoroughly designed master plan." This system clearly needed to be revised.

Difficulties arising from the lack of an effective system to monitor costs and revenues began to surface in 1978. At this time the company began losing money although, according to the firm's president, profits for the industry were at an all-time high. In 1977, profits were $190,000, but in 1978 they fell to $130,000.

Control. Traditionally, Metro had operated with a "top-down" management style in which the president oversaw the entire company's operations. By 1978, however, it was clear that Metro had grown too large for this style to be effective. At this time the president described Metro as "a collection of little offices and divisions, each working toward its own goals without considering the good of the company." It was becoming evident that because of the expansion of the company in terms of profit as well as size, the president could no longer be the sole controller of its fate.

Performance Appraisal. Metro's performance appraisal system (or lack of such a system) contributed to its retention of poor performers. Performance appraisals, when they did occur, consisted of discussions in which only positive feedback was given. There was no system for evaluating progress in terms of meeting goals, since there was no goal-setting process. Negative feedback and suggestions for improving performance were rarely given, reflecting a culture that stressed conflict avoidance.

Decision Making. Partly because of the lack of clearly defined roles and responsibilities and partly because of the traditional style of management, decisions were deferred to top management. Day-to-day decisions such as those relating to the purchase of office equipment, which should have been made by department heads or branch managers, were all presented to the president for approval. This resulted in a slow and ineffective decision-making process.

The tendency for upper management to make all decisions decreased the participation of other organization members in the decision-making process. This contributed to a lack of responsibility for actions taken and a lack of commitment to the decisions that were made. Management from the top down had been a successful way to make decisions when Metro was an entrepreneurial organization, but it had clearly become inappropriate for a firm that was ready to make a transition to professional management.

Communication. One branch manager remarked that while communication within each region was good, total company communication was poor. Communication between individual branch offices and the firm's upper management was especially ineffective. Branch managers seemed to feel that upper management was not giving them enough information for them to operate effectively. As one branch manager put it, "Upper management assumed we knew what was wanted or needed when we, in reality, didn't know."

Upper management was equally frustrated by its inability to communicate with the branch offices. As one manager put it, the lack of effective communication made it "too easy for a branch or a region to run its own shop in its own way."

Recruiting. Metro Realty did not have a formal recruiting plan, since the company had traditionally been able to attract top job candidates without expending much effort and had never experienced severe staffing problems. As the firm continued to grow, however, it found that it needed to formalize recruiting plans in order to ensure that all branch offices had an adequate number of personnel to meet the company's future goals.

In terms of recruiting, 1979 was a particularly critical year. Due to a downturn in the economy, fewer people were entering the real estate profession. It became quite evident that a recruiting plan was a necessary component of Metro's continued success.

Training and Development. Metro's major problem in the area of training and development was a lack of management development programs. Without proper training, most potential managers were not prepared to assume managerial roles. The lack of qualified managers indirectly affected the functioning of the firm.

Metro also lacked a standardized training program for sales associates. All sales associates were required to possess a state license as evidence that they had minimal competence in real estate sales, but additional training was usually needed. At Metro, each branch had traditionally offered its own on-the-job program. There was little standardization of the programs' contents, so the quality of the programs was potentially different at different branches.

Compensation. Metro's compensation system was designed to promote increased revenue at the branch level rather than profitability for the firm as a whole. The organization rewarded managers and sales associates for revenue production rather than for ability to meet financial and nonfinancial goals.

Branch managers were rewarded for the ability of their offices to generate revenue. This created certain inequities since their different locations meant that some branches automatically produced more revenue than others, regardless of the quality of the staff they employed. This compensation system led to a situation in 1978 in which two managers who possessed only marginal supervisory skills and had caused some difficulties for the organization were among the highest-paid managers in the firm.

Making the Transition

In 1978, Metro's Executive Committee, composed of the company's president, heads of the regional offices, and department heads, began to realize that the company was experiencing problems that required changes in its traditional operating systems. The committee felt that managers and brokers were too close to the situation to work adequately to resolve these problems, so it hired an independent consultant to help the firm identify and alleviate its growing pains.

In 1978, Metro began a program designed to help it make the transition to a professionally managed firm. The consultant and the company president worked together to design the program, which would be implemented over a period of four years in order to reduce employees' resistance to change. This program was designed to be evolutionary rather than revolutionary. The purpose of the effort was not "Clean the house and throw out the garbage," but rather, "Repair what we can and throw out what we find to be irreparable after we have tried to fix it."

1978. After identifying the problems described in the last section, the consultant and president began planning an organizational development program for the company. The planning process included establishing goals for the firm's transition, designing programs intended to achieve these goals, and planning how and when these programs would be implemented.

The consultant began working with the organization's members to determine what sort of company Metro would become;

that is, what the goals of the transition process would be. The group decided that the "new" organization would

1. have a decentralized system of responsibility with strong managers;
2. be managed under a participative style of leadership;
3. promote increased accountability; and
4. be profit oriented rather than strictly revenue oriented.

In order to achieve these goals, the organizational development program would focus on three major, interrelated areas: (1) organization and business planning, (2) management development, and (3) design and formalization of organization structure. Training programs in these areas would consist of lectures, group discussions, exercises, and individual counseling sessions. As the members of the organization began to put into practice what they had learned from their training, the consultant would be available to provide feedback.

The consultant and president established yearly priorities for the organizational development program. A long-term schedule was created, outlining yearly objectives and presenting suggested completion dates for various aspects of the program. This schedule is presented in Table 7.

Having outlined the goals and designed an organizational development program to meet these goals, the group devoted the latter part of 1978 to program implementation. In that year, members of the organization completed a business plan that outlined the mission, goals, objectives, and targets for the coming year (1979). This process was facilitated by giving the members training in how to design and use goals. Managers were encouraged to design goals for their individual areas of responsibility (branches, departments, or regions) as well as to contribute to the formal plan for the organization as a whole. People were also shown how to create and use a realistic budget.

Training in creating and using goals was but one part of a management development program that began to take shape in 1978. This program was intended to provide present and future

Table 7. Metro Realty Program Contents and Schedule.

1978   Plan organizational development program
             Identify problems
             Set goals
             Design programs
             Set schedule
            Begin program implementation
             Organization planning
             • Provide training in design and use of goals
             • Provide training in creation and use of budgets
             • Develop business plan for 1979
             Management development
             • Work with president to develop skills necessary to make
               personal transition
             • Work with upper management to help them develop
               skills necessary to make transition to professional
               managers
             Organization structure
             • Present exercises aimed at facilitating discussion of
               roles and responsibilities
             • Begin working toward consensus on definition of roles
1979   Review, revise, expand, and formalize programs
             Organization planning
             • Provide feedback on goals
             • Increase ability to meet goals
             • Develop more professional planning process
             Management development
             • Continue work with president
             • Expand group program to include branch managers
               and potential managers
             Organization structure
             • Formalize roles and responsibilities
             • Provide written descriptions of roles to all employees
1980–81   Continue to review, revise, expand, and formalize programs
             Organization planning
             • Make planning an integral part of the organization
             Management development
             • Continue work with president
             • Formalize program for present and potential managers
             Organization structure
             • Put formalized structure into operation

---

managers with the skills necessary to become more effective in their positions. These skills included planning, budgeting, recruiting, performance evaluation, and decision making. The consultant provided seminars in each of these areas, with practical exercises in which the new skills could be applied. He also provided feedback on performance once the skills became a part of the managers' everyday work lives.

During 1978, management development efforts were concentrated on members of upper management, though the committee planned eventually to expand the program to include all present and potential managers at Metro. The president was a member of this first group of participants, and he also worked with the consultant on an individual basis. This close working relationship was intended to help the president make his personal transition from being the leader of an entrepreneurial firm to being the CEO of a professionally managed organization. This personal transition was a key element in the success of the overall organization transition process.

The management development program initiated in 1978 served as a forum in which role ambiguities could be discussed. Exercises were used to facilitate discussion of roles and responsibilities. The consultant provided information on the need to clearly define roles and helped group members resolve role ambiguities.

1979. During this year, the programs begun in 1978 were reviewed, revised, expanded, and formalized. The planning process was refined and systematized. Regularly scheduled branch, departmental, and executive committee meetings were established to facilitate the setting of goals, objectives, and targets for the coming year. Through such meetings, goal setting became a participative process in which all organization members contributed to the formulation of the company plan. These meetings also served as a means of monitoring performance and providing feedback to the various segments of the organization.

During 1979, emphasis was placed on setting realistic financial and nonfinancial goals and working to attain these goals. The consultant provided feedback to managers on the strength of the goals they had set for their departments or branches and offered suggestions for improving their goal-setting skills.

During 1979 the firm also began to incorporate goal-setting into its performance evaluation system. Evaluations were to be based upon the extent to which employees met or exceeded the goals they had set for themselves. Compensation was to be contingent upon the ability of people to meet their goals.

Management development programs were expanded during 1979 to include existing branch managers and potential managers. The program provided branch managers with the skills they needed to be more effective in their present positions and also prepared selected branch managers for promotion to upper management positions. Selected sales associates were included in the program to ensure that the organization would have a pool of qualified potential branch managers to fill positions when needed.

By the end of the second year of the organizational development program, Metro had, for the most part, reached a consensus on role definitions. Written role descriptions were distributed to the organization's members so that there would no longer be any confusion about responsibilities.

1980-81. Review and revision of the programs begun in 1978 and 1979 continued through 1981. By 1981, people were actively participating in the planning process, which was now an integral part of the company's operating systems. Management development programs had been formalized at all levels, and role ambiguity had been minimized.

Problems Encountered

As Metro began its transition from an entrepreneurial firm to a professionally managed organization, it encountered three critical problems. One of these problems, resistance to change on the part of the organization's members, was expected. The other two problems, a severe downturn in the economy and the departure of certain key personnel from the organization, could not have been planned for. We will now further discuss these problems and their effects.

Loss of Personnel. In December 1978, one of the most successful managers at Metro left the company to form his own firm. This was a critical loss in a company that was just beginning to make the transition to a professionally managed firm, since at this point strong managers and a complete sales force are particularly needed. There is also a need for everyone to pull together, and individuals who leave a firm at this time may discourage others from supporting the change effort.

The reason for the manager's departure was not clear. He may have simply "outgrown" the organization, so that Metro was no longer meeting his needs for personal development and self-fulfillment. He may also have recognized that the organization was experiencing problems that he did not want to help in solving.

The manager made matters worse by taking quite a few salespeople with him when he left. As a result, at least two of the eleven branch offices became severely short staffed. Upper management at Metro had received little warning that this would occur. The net effect of the manager's actions was that while Metro was engaged in the already-difficult task of working to overcome its growing pains, it also faced a short-term staffing crisis and a possible accompanying drop in company morale.

The president of Metro responded quickly to the situation by rehiring Doug Perry, an experienced manager who had left the company only a year before. Perry was given the job of revitalizing the branch offices that had been devastated by staff departures. To accomplish this end, Perry took over as manager in one of the affected offices and, with the president's approval, promoted a company sales associate to the position of manager of the other affected branch. Both managers began an aggressive recruiting campaign, and within only six months the two branch offices were again fully staffed and functioning well. Because it was able to recruit quality people, Metro survived this crisis with relatively little adverse impact on its efforts to become a professionally managed firm.

Declining Economy. Having survived this staffing crisis, Metro suffered another blow in 1979 when the economy experienced a severe downturn. Real estate sales dropped suddenly and unexpectedly because of unprecedentedly high interest rates, vanishing mortgage funds, and uncertainty about the future.

The president of Metro suggested that this downturn was merely part of a cycle that occurs every few years. He pointed out, "This cycle begins with a period of prosperity like that which occurred in the late 1970s. Assuming that real estate is one of the best hedges against inflation, many people begin to buy houses left and right with the expectation that they can make profits without running any risks. This type of speculation cannot continue indefinitely. It eventually results in a declining market like that of 1979–80." At such times, he noted, weaker firms begin to fail as salespeople leave not only the firms but the industry itself and new people fail to enter the profession.

Nonetheless, the shift in the economy that occurred in 1979–80 was one of the most severe downturns the real estate market had experienced. The economic shift was especially threatening to Metro because it occurred when the company was just beginning to make the transition to a professionally managed firm. In response to this threat, the president took the stance that Metro could be a "victim" or it could take advantage of the market. He chose the latter course of action and adopted a strategy that was intended to play on the strengths of Metro and concentrate on the long term, making the most of opportunities. This strategy would allow Metro to respond when the market changed.

Metro Realty was fortunate in that it had a strong image in its community and also in that its management had prepared itself for possible economic downturns by designing contingency plans. The plan that the company adopted in 1979–80 promoted both cost containment and production. It also emphasized maintaining the sales force, since in such periods there are fewer people entering the industry, and qualified people are at a premium.

All managers were asked to contribute ideas about specific expenses to cut, but the president had the final say in this effort. He decided that advertising budgets would be fixed, charitable contributions would be suspended, greater control of expense reimbursement to sales associates would be instituted, a freeze would be placed on the hiring of management and salaried personnel, and closing of nonproductive branch offices would be considered.

The company's strategy apparently paid off, since, despite market conditions, the company's performance in 1980 was one of the best in its forty-two year history.

Resistance to Change. Even after people realized that there were problems with the old operating systems at Metro, some individuals refused to take part in the changes necessary to solve these problems. They seemed to have a great desire to cling to old values and operating procedures. They showed their resistance to change in a variety of ways, including excuses for not adapting to procedures, justifications for using old practices, complaints that the changes were taking away the "family atmosphere" that people treasured, and, ultimately, outright refusals to adopt the new values and practices.

Some managers complained, "I just can't do it that way." The consultant replied, "Yes, you can, if you try"—and the president added, "You *will* do it that way." People who absolutely would not change were finally asked to leave since they were detracting from the transition process. By 1981, after a certain amount of struggle, most employee resistance had been reduced through adoption of the new strategy or through elimination of the chief resisters. It now appeared that Metro Realty had, for the most part, successfully made the transition to a professionally managed firm.

Program Outcomes

Metro Realty's organizational development program was successful in helping the company make the transition from an entrepreneurship to a professionally managed firm, even in the face of the problems that were encountered. Fundamental changes in the organization, shown in Table 8, eliminated most of its "growing pains."

Culture. One of the most difficult changes Metro had to make was to replace its "family atmosphere" with an atmosphere that was more conducive to accomplishing the tasks of a professionally managed firm. This meant that managers had to learn how to confront conflict and eliminate poor performers. It did not necessarily mean that "a family feeling" could no longer exist. However, the dysfunctional aspects of this part of the firm's culture had to be eliminated.

Another component of the culture, the definition of productivity, also had to be changed. Individual productivity in the "new" organization was to be assessed in terms of profit contributed

Table 8. The "Old" and "New" Metro.

	Old	New
Culture	Poor performers are tolerated.	Poor performers are not tolerated.
	The company is a "family."	The notion of "family" remains but is modified.
	Managers avoid conflict.	Managers are able to deal with conflict.
	Productivity is loosely defined.	Productivity is closely related to profitability.
	Company concentrates on revenue production.	Company concentrates on profit production.
Roles and Responsibilities	Roles and responsibilities are not cleary defined.	Roles and responsibilities are clearly defined.
	Responsibilities often overlap.	Responsibilities are mutually agreed upon and do not overlap.
	Role confusion causes frustration.	Written definitions distributed to all employees eliminate confusion.
Planning	No formal business plan exists.	A formal planning process becomes an integral part of the organization.
	Company has no formalized goals, objectives, or mission.	Managers are taught how to design and use goals, and regularly scheduled meetings are used to evaluate progress towards goals.
	Little direction is given to personnel.	Personnel are asked to participate in planning a course of action for the company.
Budgets and Accounting System	No formalized budget exists; budget process is only an "exercise."	Managers design and use realistic budgets.
	Financial information is available only for the entire company.	A new accounting system provides information for all levels of the company in a timely manner.
	Information available is often inaccurate or incomplete.	
	Accounting system is underdeveloped.	
Organization Control	Top-down management style is used.	Participative management style is used.

Table 8. The "Old" and "New" Metro, Cont'd.

	Old	*New*
	Control is often ineffective.	Regularly scheduled meetings monitor performance and provide feedback.
Performance Appraisal	Appraisal consists of discussion between managers and subordinates.	Employees are evaluated on progress toward goals.
	Only positive feedback is given; little effort is made to improve performance.	Supervisors provide both positive and negative feedback and ways to improve performance.
Decision Making	Most decisions are made by top management; decision making is slow and often ineffective.	Decision-making responsibility is distributed throughout the organization.
	Lack of participation in decisions leads to lack of commitment to decisions made.	Planning process encourages maximum participation by all employees.
Communication	Total company communication is poor; communication between upper management and branch managers is most ineffective.	Clearly defined roles and responsibilities contribute to better communication.
	Poor communication contributes to branch managers' role confusion and control by upper management.	Regularly scheduled meetings increase communication between various levels of the organization.
Recruiting	No formal recruiting plan exists.	Recruiting is a planned activity.
	With a growing number of branches, staffing is becoming a problem.	Managers are evaluated partly on their ability to set and meet recruiting goals.
Training and Development	No management development program exists.	Formal management development program exists.
	No standardized training for sales associates exists.	Training department is responsible for training of sales associates.
Compensation	Compensation is based on ability of branch to generate revenue.	Compensation is based on ability of personnel to meet financial and nonfinancial goals.

to the firm. This meant that people not only had to increase revenues; they also had to control costs. Something like mailing flyers could no longer be considered productive work in itself, but only as it contributed to the overall profitability of the branch and firm. If any activity was judged too costly in terms of the revenue it was expected to generate, it would be eliminated.

Profitability was also important in the evaluation of branch productivity. The Executive Committee decided that in the "new" organization, each branch would be regarded as a profit center instead of simply a revenue center. The goal of each branch manager thus was to have a profitable branch, which meant continuing to produce high revenues while controlling and being responsible for expenses. Profitability would become a measure of managerial success and the management development program would help managers achieve this success by providing them with the skills they needed to be effective professional managers.

Roles and Responsibilities. Through the lectures, discussions, and exercises used in the management development program, the organization structure of Metro was defined. Roles and responsibilities of position holders and formal links between various positions were identified, formalized, and distributed in written form to all employees so that there would no longer be any confusion about who was responsible for what.

Planning. Systems for planning were formalized. The organization developed an ongoing means of setting, monitoring, and evaluating goals. This included a series of branch, departmental, and executive committee meetings that facilitated the setting of goals, objectives, and targets for the coming year. The meetings also helped in evaluating progress towards goals. An important part of the planning process was the use of contingency plans, whereby the firm attempted to determine what strategy to adopt in an optimistic or pessimistic market. Such planning helped the company weather the severe economic environment of 1979–80, when many less well prepared companies failed.

Budgets and Accounting System. Organization members' ability to design and use budgets was developed through seminars presented by the consultant. In the first year or two that managers attempted to use the techniques described in these seminars, nearly all the branch managers failed to meet their budgets because of either unrealistic goals or inadequate monitoring of goals. By 1981, however, managers had become better able to meet their financial as well as nonfinancial goals.

To further promote this process, Metro implemented a new accounting system. In the new system, information was available on each level of the organization, from the organization as a whole to each region to the individual branch offices. There was initially a problem with the timeliness of the reports: information was not being received at a rate conducive to effective monitoring of financial goals. In 1980, however, this problem was reduced when a computerized accounting system was installed. The new system increased the speed with which financial reports could be generated and distributed.

Control. A series of regularly scheduled meetings replaced the "top-down" management style as a means of control. These meetings helped to monitor performance and provide feedback to various segments of the organization, thus also serving to increase communication.

Executive committee meetings were held monthly. Members of this group, along with branch managers, formed the "planning committee," which met quarterly to prepare priorities and nonfinancial objectives and to review plans and status reports. Department and branch meetings were also to be held monthly to review the status of goal achievement. Annual planning meetings, in which all branch managers, department heads, regional managers, and administrative personnel were involved, were to be held in June and July of each year.

Performance Appraisal. A performance review system based on goal achievement was created. Evaluation sessions were designed to provide feedback (both positive and negative) to each employee on his or her performance and to provide specific direction for improvement in the coming year. Managers' performance was assessed according to how well they met their goals in profit, recruiting, training, planning, control, turnover, and reliability. Sales associates' performance was assessed in terms of performance toward goals in sales, number of contracts, open houses, and other areas deemed important by the individual manager and sales associate. Goals for all employees were established through mutual agreement between employee and supervisor and were to be congruent with the overall company goals.

Decision Making. One purpose of defining roles and responsibilities was to distribute decision-making responsibility to various levels throughout the organization—to decentralize responsibility, in other words. The president would no longer be responsible for all company decisions. Instead, managers would make the day-to-day decisions for their individual branches, regions, or departments.

The formal planning process developed at Metro allowed an even greater number of people to have a voice in the decisions that affected the company. The process was designed to encourage maximum participation by the organization's members. All those involved were to have input into decisions that would directly affect them.

Communication. Clarification of roles and responsibilities, along with establishment of regular meetings, eliminated many of the communication problems that Metro had experienced. The company now had a clearly defined "chain of command" through which information could filter both down and up.

Recruiting. As part of the yearly plan, each branch manager was to set goals for the number of individuals he or she would recruit in the coming year. Each manager was also to devise an action plan for meeting these goals. Managers were encouraged to seek new employees at local junior colleges, through business contracts, or even at other firms. Part of each manager's performance appraisal was an evaluation of success in meeting recruiting goals.

Training and Development. In an effort to provide continuing education, Metro established a training department that was responsible for all programs given to Metro employees. The head of this department was to work with each branch to design programs that would meet the needs of the individual branch offices and the organization at large. The training department was therefore able to control the quality of the programs offered to employees and to ensure that all employees received sufficient training. As described previously, Metro also developed a formal management development program to help individuals become professional managers and to create a pool of potential managers.

Compensation. The objective of the new compensation system was to reduce the emphasis on increasing the revenues of individual branches and replace this with an emphasis on increasing the profit of the organization as a whole. To achieve this end, managers were to be rewarded for meeting or exeeding financial and nonfinancial goals. Common costs were to be allocated to branches and departments in proportion to their ability to generate revenues, thus reducing inequities in revenue generation between various branch locations.

Under the new system, each manager would receive a base salary plus a certain percentage of the company's profit, based on the extent to which that manager's branch had met or exceeded its financial goals. Such a system encouraged managers to exercise care in establishing budgets. It also offered managers an incentive to meet or exceed budgets, thus increasing the profit of the firm as a whole.

The results of Metro Realty's organizational development program suggest that the company was successful at meeting the goals it had set for its transition.

1. The company now had a decentralized system of responsibility: branch, department, and regional managers were responsible for setting and meeting their own goals.
2. Participative leadership was becoming a reality: All managers took part in a yearly planning process for their individual areas of responsibility and for the company as a whole. The president no longer had the ultimate decision-making responsibility.
3. Accountability had been increased: All employees were held accountable for meeting the goals they had set for themselves, and compensation was based upon their ability to do so.
4. The organization had become profit oriented: The culture had been changed to emphasize profit rather than revenue. Rewards were based upon ability to generate profit for the company rather than simply revenue for the branch.

Conclusion

Although Metro Realty happened to be a real estate company, its transition from stage II to stage III was typical of many companies in a variety of industries. As companies expand and begin to experience growing pains, farsighted managers like those at Metro Realty recognize the need for a change and begin to develop and formalize the management systems needed to overcome these problems. To create these systems, they design and implement an organizational development program something like that used at Metro Realty.

At Metro, the development program had three parts: organization design, organization planning, and management development. Each of these parts met a specific developmental need. The organization design component was intended to help Metro develop a formal organization structure in which people understood their roles, responsibilities, and reporting relationships. The organization planning process taught employees how to formulate financial and nonfinancial goals and help the company develop systems for setting, monitoring, and evaluating these goals. Through developing monitoring systems (such as performance appraisals and a budgeting system), Metro also created a control system. The management development component of the organization development program helped present and potential managers be more effective in their roles.

Developing management systems can take a number of years, and there can be many obstacles to overcome, as happened at Metro Realty. However, if an organization is to continue to be successful as it grows, its management must recognize that problems exist and begin taking steps towards reducing them, no matter how painful the process may be.

The case of Metro Realty teaches a number of lessons about making the transition from an entrepreneurship (stage I or II) to a professionally managed firm (stage III). The first lesson is that growing pains like those experienced by Metro are unavoidable. Entrepreneurial firms that are successful and therefore grow rapidly can expect to experience certain problems related to the fact that they haven't had time to develop effective management systems.

Other areas of the company have, justifiably, required more attention.

The second lesson is that management must recognize the symptoms of organizational growing pains and realize that it is time for a change. Management and others may prefer to ignore the problems or blame them on some fluke because no one wants to admit that the company's success is threatened. Some people may believe that the problems will disappear if the company keeps operating in the manner that has proven effective in the past. But this belief, as we saw in Chapter Four, can cause the organization to fall victim to the Osborne syndrome.

The third lesson is that the needed changes can be quite painful for those involved. People desire to cling to familiar, traditional ways of operating. Formalization of roles, responsibilities, planning, and control suggests to many people that the "warm" atmosphere of the entrepreneurial firm is being replaced by "cold" professionalism. Whether or not this actually occurs, management must remain steadfast in its efforts to transform the organization.

The final lesson to be learned from Metro Realty is that the transition process cannot be accomplished overnight; indeed, it may take years. This need for slowness is, in fact, an asset. Introducing change slowly can help to reduce employee resistance and anxiety. It is also important to help employees understand why changes are being made so they do not feel threatened and will know what to expect in the future.

This chapter has attempted to show how an organization can recognize the need for management systems and set about developing them. This critical challenge must be met if the organization is to make a successful transition from entrepreneurship to professionally managed firm.

6

⚜⚜⚜

The Consolidation
Stage: Managing
the Corporate Culture

After a company has successfully professionalized its management systems, it must meet a further developmental challenge that involves making very different types of changes. At this point the organization has reached stage IV, and its main task becomes the formalization of its corporate culture.

As we explained in Chapter One, corporate culture consists of the values, beliefs, and norms that govern the behavior of people in an organization. The culture reflects what the organization stands for in its products or services, the management of its people, and the way it conducts business. Culture can have a profound impact on an organization's success or failure. It can determine the degree of employee commitment to a firm and affect the way customers perceive the enterprise.

During a firm's early stages of growth, culture is transmitted informally through employees' day-to-day interactions with the entrepreneur. As the firm grows, however, the entrepreneur tends to have less time for contact with an ever-increasing number of people. Accordingly, unless a formal mechanism is substituted for the process of cultural transmission by osmosis, the firm will find that its people no longer have a shared vision of what the company is or where it is going. (The creation of a shared vision for a company is part of the managerial function of strategic leadership, which will be examined in Chapter Ten.)

By the time a firm reaches stage IV, the lack of a shared culture can produce a number of problems. Individuals are left to create their own cultures, which may not always be in the best interest of the whole company. Thus a formal program for auditing the corporate culture and disseminating it to peer groups of employees becomes a necessity.

This chapter will show the impact of corporate culture on the development of a successful stage IV firm. Its example case history will demonstrate how culture changes in unintended ways as a company grows, what problems arise as a result of those changes, and how an organization can manage cultural changes in a way that lets it become a successful stage IV company.

As with Metro Realty, our example company actually exists, but we have changed its name and certain facts in its situation to preserve its confidentiality.

Tempo Products Unlimited: Background

From very modest beginnings, Tempo Products Unlimited (TPU) grew into a large, successful consumer products corporation with revenues exceeding \$150 million.* Much of the firm's initial success could be attributed to its owner, Ronald Harrison, who was willing to take certain risks that allowed his company to grow and prosper.

In 1971, Ron Harrison founded Tempo Products Unlimited, a consumer products manufacturing company. This firm was small in employees, size, and revenues, and it manufactured only one product, which appealed to a limited audience.

The first few years of Ron's ownership involved constant struggle. Sales were not bad, but they could have been better. The company was not growing, though it seemed to be maintaining its

* The actual numbers and certain other facts have been changed to preserve the company's confidentiality. I have also exercised editorial license to select those aspects of the history of this company that are most pertinent to the theme of this chapter.

market share. The turning point for TPU came when Ron and his small staff decided to implement some new product ideas and marketing strategies. These changes were very effective at increasing sales. By 1975, the company had revenues totaling $5 million and included about sixty people on its staff.

In 1978, Ron concluded that it was time for his company to expand further. Since he had had great success with the new product line, he decided to invest in other products that might appeal to his target audience. He added two new products to the existing ones, and both met with great success. Ron and his company seemed to be doing everything right.

In the ensuing years, Ron invested in a few other selected products aimed at his target audience. By 1980, total company revenues were $100 million, and by 1983 they totaled more than $150 million. Personnel had increased to 650 in 1983. This rapid growth was very much the result of the entrepreneurial skills Ron Harrison possessed: the ability to identify a market niche, the ability to create and produce a product appropriate for that niche, the willingness to take risks, and the ability to attract talented people to assist him in building his enterprise. In brief, Ron was a classic entrepreneur.

Elements of TPU's Culture and Their Attenuation

Tempo Products Unlimited had been successful at creating most of the operating systems it needed to remain profitable as it grew. Its accounting system and control system were reasonably well developed and were operating effectively. The company had implemented a planning system and was continuing to formalize it. In 1980, however, the firm's management realized that problems unrelated to operating systems were arising. These problems proved to be the result of unintended reinterpretations of the values, norms, and beliefs that had served the company well during its growth. TPU's original culture, management realized, was in the process of attenuating.

When TPU was small, Ron was the source of its corporate culture. He relied on close interaction with employees to disseminate his beliefs and his vision for the company's future. As the company grew, however, such interaction was no longer possible, and the company's culture became increasingly unclear to new generations of employees. Some of these employees therefore began to create their own values, beliefs, and norms. At times, this new culture was at odds with TPU's original culture.

As differing and sometimes opposing values, beliefs, and norms were translated into action, conflicts arose. People lacked a shared perception of what the company was and where it was going. As one manager said, "We don't know what business we're in. We have many employees who don't know what type of products we make." This form of "growing pains" typically occurs at about the time a company is ready to make the transition from a stage III to a stage IV firm.

Changes in certain elements of TPU's culture were particularly important. Let us take a look at these elements as they existed in the original company culture and then see how they were becoming attenuated.

TPU is a family. The culture at TPU had traditionally emphasized a "family atmosphere." In the company's early years, everyone knew everyone else, and everyone pulled together for a common cause: the success of the firm. This corporate-wide family feeling was easy to maintain because most employees interacted with one another on a regular basis and also were able to interact directly with Ron, who provided the guidance needed to keep people working together effectively. However, as the firm began its rapid growth, the "family" became less cohesive because the size of the company made it impossible to have the number of interactions necessary to sustain it. This dissolution of a "family feeling" is a common occurrence in rapidly growing entrepreneurial firms.

At TPU, an employee's organizational "family" became redefined as either those who were of the same "generation" or those with whom the employee worked most closely. There were two generations of employees at TPU. The older one entered the firm in the years prior to its period of rapid growth (before 1975), while the new generation entered TPU after 1975.

The older generation of employees came to believe that they were the "true family members," the ones who had really built the company. They considered the new generation to be outsiders. Consequently, members of the older generation, many of whom occupied middle and senior management positions, believed that they were entitled to certain privileges that the new generation of employees should not receive. These privileges included access to people, information, and other resources.

This belief was supported, at least in part, by the emphasis that TPU's management placed on the use of confidential information. Only "family" members—that is, management—were entitled to such information, and members of the new generation who were denied access to it came to resent not being "in" on company activities and decisions. They responded by creating their own "family grapevine" through which they could circulate information. Management in turn came to resent the fact that, in reality, there was no confidential information; it was readily available to most employees through this informal system of corporate communication.

An individual's work group also became a "family." This made sense because interaction among individuals in a work group is usually high, so people have a good chance to create satisfying relationships. This definition of "family" was also influenced by the structure that evolved as TPU grew.

During the company's early development, its structure had been loose. As more products and personnel were added, however, a more formal structure developed, with its basis in the various functions of the company. Each area, such as production or sales, came to see itself in isolation from all other areas. This "separate islands syndrome" led to duplication of services and inefficiencies within the organization. It also replaced the total "family" feeling with a feeling of identification mainly with the work group. As a result, employees began to experience conflicting loyalties. "Do I work for my group or for the corporation?" became a prevalent question. It was often answered with "I work only for my group."

Decision-makers are few and invincible. Ron Harrison, as founder and owner, had obviously been responsible for providing the vision of what TPU was to become. In TPU's early years, this involved making most of the company's decisions and providing direction to employees. Employees accepted the fact that it was Ron's responsibility to make decisions involving his investment, and they supported him in whatever course of action he chose. The belief was that, as one manager put it: "Ron will decide. He knows what he wants the company to be. I don't worry about it because it's all in his head."

People wanted Ron to make the decisions because he had the uncanny ability to "always make the right one." This ability created the belief that Ron was somehow invincible, a superman that no one could surpass. The company's spectacular success reinforced this belief.

As TPU grew, the decision-making ability and "invincibility" that Ron alone had originally been thought to possess became attributed, through a halo effect, to anyone who occupied a senior management position. Thus the belief became "Senior management will decide; they know what's right."

Because of this belief, it became an accepted practice to defer most decisions to senior management, even when the decisions could have been made at a lower level in the company. Inefficiencies resulted from this practice for three reasons. First, senior managers were no longer able to make rational decisions on some matters because they were too far removed from the daily activities that their decisions would affect. Their decisions were, therefore, sometimes inappropriate and sometimes made too slowly to be of value.

The second reason why inefficiencies arose was that deferring decisions to the upper levels of the company allowed lower-level managers to avoid responsibility for decisions that affected them or their areas. If lower-level managers failed to reach a goal set for them by senior management, they could claim that they were not accountable because "it was not my decision."

A final reason for inefficiencies was an excessive dependence on outside consultants. This was costly in terms of both time and money. Consultants seemed to be used in instances where decisions should have been made by the managers themselves. According to some people in the company, consultants were used so often because upper managers did not want to take responsibility for their own decisions.

In fact, senior managers came to deny that they had sole decision-making responsibility. They created policies suggesting that lower-level personnel should be involved in decision making. In practice, however, lower-level managers were still controlled and restrained by upper management's decisions. For example, one person said of TPU's budget process, "It lacks credibility because budget cuts are issued from the top after the budget is approved. This is seen as a mockery of the system, since people aren't given decision-making responsibility."

The lack of decision-making responsibilities made some managers feel powerless and therefore do nothing at all. As one person pointed out, "There are too many managers who have no real authority because someone else can rule over them." This situation frustrated managers who were supposed to be invested with authority, but complaints seldom reached upper management because the notion of upper management's invincibility had come to mean that people should not challenge their superiors. Doing so was likely to result in adverse personal consequences.

This fear of reprisals for "making waves" contributed to the adoption of a "top-down" communication system that provided little opportunity for lower-level employees to communicate their ideas to upper management. In fact, it almost prohibited such communication. One employee said, "Subordinates tell managers what they want to hear, not necessarily what they believe."

Afraid to voice opposition, most lower-level managers simply accepted the need to seek direction for future activities from senior management and to do as they were told. One person described the situation this way: "Always being on the outside, doing just what you're told without explanations or understanding of long-range goals, gives employees the idea that they are a commodity and not a resource."

"Whatever it takes, get it done with excellence." One of the beliefs on which TPU was founded was that its products should be of the highest quality. People believed that Ron was willing to devote whatever resources were necessary to reach this goal. Cost was less important than the desire to produce excellent products. An implicit motto at TPU was "Whatever it takes, get it done with excellence."

It appeared to both employees and outsiders that Ron also believed that to create excellent products, one must employ excellent people. This in turn fostered the belief that Ron was willing to spend more than his competitors to attract and keep such people. TPU employees believed that they were paid above the industry average. At least one person suggested, in fact, that TPU employees were spoiled by excessive rewards.

Ron's stressing of excellence in products and people had created a positive image of TPU in the eyes of both employees and outsiders and had made a major contribution to the company's success.

As TPU grew, however, these positive values came to be misinterpreted. The goal of product excellence came to mean "We are a first-class organization." This in turn was interpreted to mean "We always go first class." The implicit corollary of this was "Cost does not matter."

The goal of excellence in people was also misinterpreted. People came to believe that they could not help performing well, and they expected rewards regardless of what their actual performance was. The standard of employee excellence was redefined to mean "Whatever a TPU employee does is excellent."

Our company is unique. TPU employees believed that their company was unique in both its good and its bad attributes. This belief was supported by policies and practices that Ron had created to help employees feel "special" and thus increase pride and motivation.

Unfortunately, as the company grew, this belief led to problems at the organizational level. TPU employees came to feel that the company's excellence rested on its "uniqueness" and that treating it like any other company would therefore jeopardize its survival. They believed that TPU was so unique, in fact, that it would not learn from the lessons of others. They complained about the proposed use of organization development methods that had proven successful elsewhere because "they won't work at a company like ours" and "we can figure out our own problems." The belief in "excellence through uniqueness" thus came to be used as a way to protect people against change and to excuse their resistance to modification attempts.

"Play it by ear." TPU's early success was partly due to its ability to change to meet environmental requirements—to "play it by ear." Formal roles and responsibilities, a planning system, and well-defined operating systems did not exist in the early years, nor

were they necessary for the company's success. TPU and its employees operated on a day-to-day basis, making whatever adjustments they needed to carve out a market niche. This was a very effective approach in an entrepreneurial firm, since it allowed for rapid change.

As the company grew, however, the practice of "playing it by ear" became dysfunctional. TPU's management realized that the company could no longer successfully operate on an informal basis and began taking steps towards formalizing its management and operating systems. Specifically, the firm became concerned with three levels of problems resulting from the "play it by ear" belief.

At the individual level, the belief meant that some employees did not have clearly defined roles and responsibilities. As the firm grew, role definitions were made for some positions but not others. Many of the positions that remained ill defined had been created when the company needed additional employees to cope with its rapid growth. Since TPU's management was relatively young and inexperienced, it had tended to add people without trying to reconceptualize the functions being performed or the organizational structure required to perform them. Ambiguous role definitions contributed to productivity problems when employees unknowingly worked at odds with corporate goals or did nothing at all. Furthermore, individuals in these positions sometimes believed that they could not be held accountable for their actions because their roles had not been defined.

At the management level, informality contributed to problems in communication. When TPU was a small company, informal communication met both employee and company needs. As the firm grew, however, the need for a formal communication system became apparent—but one was not created, because of the desire to cling to the old value of "playing it by ear." The lack of a formal system contributed to inefficiencies in production, duplication of effort, and misunderstandings between divisions.

At the organizational level, it became clear that the lack of a formal planning process and a clearly articulated culture were causing problems. Each division within the company was able to design a strategic plan for itself, but these plans were often formulated without considering the needs of other areas. Similarly, each area had its own financial and nonfinancial goals, and these sometimes conflicted with the goals of other areas. An integrated strategic plan was needed so that employees could understand and focus on company goals rather than just the goals of their particular work area.

Have fun. While TPU's culture stressed working to achieve excellence, it also emphasized that people should enjoy their work. This element of the company's culture was based on Ron's desire to create a pleasant work environment to balance the uncertainty that is unavoidable in growing, entrepreneurial firms. As Ron said, "I've tried to establish a spirit that we shouldn't take ourselves too seriously; we should have fun. You need to relieve the pressure of not knowing what the future holds."

Unfortunately, as the company grew, Ron's belief that people should have fun became transformed into a mandate that all employees *"will* have fun." In practice, this meant avoidance of conflict, since people believed that conflict was disruptive and not good for the company or its personnel. Avoiding conflict with senior managers became particularly important, since they could punish those who challenged them. It was also important, however, to avoid conflict with one's peers and subordinates—not to "make waves." According to one manager, it was generally accepted that "the best way to get fired is to talk too much" and that "80 percent of the terminations are people who made waves across organization lines."

Managers believed that it was better to avoid conflict with their subordinates than to disrupt the system by providing negative feedback or dismissing poor performers. One manager remarked that when subordinates were criticized, they either "cried or made excuses." Many managers therefore came to believe that it was better to say nothing at all. This contributed to retention of poor performers.

Do your own thing and do it well. One belief that had existed at TPU from its inception was that people should be allowed to find their own levels of performance and that if excellence in products and work environment was stressed, every employee's standard would be high. In the company's early years, "Do your own thing and do it well" was carried out in practice as employees devoted a great deal of energy to making the company a success. Employees were motivated to achieve the standard of excellence implicit in "do it well" because they were encouraged by others and, most important, by Ron to "do their best." A high degree of interaction between Ron and his employees increased motivation, and in adequate performers could be easily identified and dealt with. The high degree of interaction also created a feeling of togetherness, so people's "own thing" usually fitted in with the goals of the company. As the organization grew, however, people grew apart both physically and psychologically, and "Do your own thing" became distorted at three levels.

At the individual level, employees came to interpret "Do your own thing" as "Do what is best for yourself." This sometimes meant doing nothing at all, as suggested by one manager: "People don't work around here anymore. They loaf, visit, chat, or wander the halls." This distortion grew partly out of the lack of a clearly articulated culture, partly out of the lack of formally defined roles and responsibilities, and partly out of the belief that conflict should be avoided at all costs. Without a well-defined and clearly communicated culture, it became acceptable to interpret "do your own thing" in many ways. Ambiguous roles led some employees to believe that they could create their own positions without considering the goals of the company. Furthermore, some employees became so frustrated by the lack of formal responsibilities or the overlap between their roles and others' that they just gave up and did nothing at all. Such behavior was allowed to continue because challenging it might result in conflict, and the culture stressed that conflict should be avoided.

At the managerial level, "Do your own thing" came to mean that managers could choose the leadership style that best met their personal, but not necessarily the company's needs. Managers differed in ability to delegate and make decisions, and those with well-developed leadership skills were sometimes dependent on those who did not have such skills. Effective managers thus often became frustrated because they were unable to attain their goals. One person noted, "There are many different leadership and management styles among TPU managers, and this has tended to create uneven delegation of responsibility and unclear decision making." The culture was not strong enough to support the adoption of effective styles of management, nor was there an institutionalized management development program in which managers could learn the skills they needed to be effective in their jobs.

At the organizational level, one interpretation of "Do your own thing" gave support to the "separate islands syndrome." Each area came to believe that in order to fulfill its needs, it had to compete with other areas for resources. This led individual areas to become highly protective of their territories. Relatedly, area managers often believed that if "outsiders" (such as consultants) were able to audit their operations, they might lose resources and even their jobs. The cultural belief became "Do your own thing, but stay out of my territory."

In response to this fear, communication between areas became minimal. Some employees, in fact, said that horizontal communication at TPU was practically nonexistent. Lack of communication resulted in duplication of effort between divisions and a reduction in the ability of areas to work together effectively. For example, on one occasion production manufactured more of a product than the service center could store. The product had to be stored elsewhere, resulting in unanticipated costs. Production had failed to communicate its needs to the service center because the company's culture discouraged horizontal communication in the interest of "protecting one's territory."

Redefining a Culture

In 1980, TPU's senior management began to realize that certain aspects of the company's culture needed to be changed if it was to continue to be successful. Ron Harrison therefore worked with others to create an organizational development program to help TPU redefine its culture. The program was to emphasize four broad areas: (1) organization design; (2) strategic planning; (3) management development; and (4) culture management.

Organization Design. As TPU grew, its structure remained relatively unchanged. This lack of structural change, combined with certain cultural elements, resulted in a number of "growing pains." For example, when combined with the cultural element of "do your own thing," the company's obsolete structure led to the "separate islands syndrome."

TPU's managers recognized the need for organization redesign. They realized that the design process not only should aim to alleviate current problems but also should plan for the company's next stage of development in order to avoid future problems.

It became evident to Ron Harrison that the company's redesign should include some changes in leadership. During TPU's first stages of development, Ron's unique skills as a risk taker, investor, and market niche identifier had contributed greatly to the company's success. This type of leadership is termed "strategic leadership" (see Chapter Ten). Ron realized, however, that the $150 million company that TPU had become required different leadership skills for its continued success. At this stage of development, TPU needed a leader who was skilled at maintaining its day-to-day operations. This type of leadership is termed "operational leadership." As will be explained in Chapter Ten, Ron had two alternatives in meeting this need: develop the required skills himself or hire someone who had the skills that he had not adequately developed.

After much discussion with experts and consideration of the matter, Ron decided that his company's and his own needs would best be met if someone else were appointed to run TPU on a day-to-day basis. Ron could then assume the role of Chief Executive and remain responsible for strategic planning, new ventures, and organizational development. In 1982, therefore, Ron appointed Stewart Page, an advisor to TPU for a number of years, to the office of president. Stewart was selected because he was familiar with the business and because Ron believed he could get the type of results that the company needed.

The change in leadership was communicated to employees through both word and action. The word consisted of a formal announcement of Page's appointment, and the action consisted of a number of changes in policy and practice that symbolized a change in the company's culture as well as a change in leadership.

Stewart Page made his presence felt almost immediately by reducing the company's "deadwood" in two ways. First, he asked people who had been "doing their own thing" without regard for the company's benefit to leave. Second, he analyzed positions for their contributions to the overall functioning of the firm, and positions that appeared to have no clear responsibilities and did not serve a critical function for the company were eliminated. Employees who occupied these positions were either terminated or relocated. During this period "heads rolled."

After the deadwood had been eliminated, a new and more formalized organization chart that clearly depicted how different positions related to one another was developed. Job descriptions were reviewed and revised, or created, to accommodate the changes made in the organization's structure. These new definitions of roles and responsibilities were communicated to employees both formally and informally so that all would clearly understand the way their jobs related to the total company's functioning.

Stewart Page also promoted cost control. He made it clear that the company would no longer tolerate excessive spending and that managers would be held accountable for their budgets.

Stewart set about reducing the "separate islands syndrome" by increasing communication across organization lines. He did this by creating a company-wide operating committee that brought together individuals from various divisions within the company. This group also increased communication between middle and upper management by acting as the liaison between senior management and the rest of the organization.

Eventually, Stewart hoped to create operating committees for each product division. These committees would be responsible for setting, monitoring, and evaluating the division's goals. The creation of these committees was intended to move the organization's structure toward a focus on "profit centers" with functional general managers.

Through these actions and others, the change in leadership and the change in culture that it represented were communicated to TPU's employees. It became clear that several aspects of the old culture, including "playing it by ear," "doing your own thing," and operating in isolation from other areas of the company, were gone forever. The company was going to develop the culture of a professional firm, which included more formalized operating systems, conforming "your own thing" with the company's interests, and working together in an integrated, cooperative fashion.

Strategic Planning. TPU had begun to implement a corporate planning process in the late 1970s, but this process had not been institutionalized and was not functioning effectively. In 1980, senior management became aware that a more formal corporate plan was needed and set about creating one. (For a complete discussion of strategic planning, see Chapter Seven.)

The first challenge the company faced was to decide what business it was in. Creating a corporate identity is the first step in defining a corporate culture and designing a strategic plan. TPU had grown into a company with five divisions related to different products, and it lacked focus. Upper management therefore worked to clarify the company's identity through meetings and discussions outlining its present and future business growth opportunities. Corporate leaders eventually decided that TPU was in the business of producing small consumer items designed for the tastes of a special market segment.

Once this mission statement was agreed upon, management began to create a strategic plan and to formalize the strategic planning process. Stewart Page established a planning department to concentrate on the long-term growth and goals of TPU and integrate the plans of various divisions.

Management Development. TPU had traditionally offered management development opportunities to its employees, but it had never had a formalized training program. Thus the quality of management training varied from year to year, depending on its frequency, content, and instructors.

Stewart Page and his senior managers recognized the need for formalized and continuing training programs. A belief in such programs was consistent with Ron Harrison's view that the key resource of TPU was people and that training could help to increase the value of this resource. Stewart, however, saw that these programs could also serve as a means of redefining and communicating the company's culture.

Both Ron and Stewart believed that it was important for members of upper management to understand and be able to perform their responsibilities effectively. Since the company's existing management training programs appeared to be insufficient, TPU's leaders asked an independent consultant to help them design new training programs for senior management. These programs consisted of counseling and skill-building sessions overseen by a professional trainer.

Stewart also recognized the need to improve the training programs offered to middle managers. Traditionally, these programs were not formal and attendance at them was not required. Thus, the quality of managers' training varied greatly. Stewart decided that the company needed a more formalized management development program that was precisely tailored to TPU's unique qualities and problems.

Working with an independent consultant, Stewart and other members of upper management developed a program that both provided training to present and potential managers and helped the company redefine and communicate its culture. The program consisted of lectures, readings, structured exercises, and group discussions, all focusing on the unique aspects and skill requirements of being a manager at TPU. (An in-depth example of the use of a management development program in a company facing issues similar to those at TPU is presented in Chapter Nine.)

Initially only selected middle managers participated in these programs, although the programs were intended to eventually include all present and potential managers. This gradual implementation allowed the programs to be tested for their ability to meet the company's needs. It also helped to reduce participants' potential resistance to change.

Stewart hoped for three important outcomes from these management development programs. First, they should create a pool of skilled managers. Second, since participants were drawn from different areas of the company, he hoped that the shared experience of taking part in the programs would create lasting relationships that could serve as linking pins between areas of the company. Finally, he hoped that program participants would bring back to their areas both new skills and the new definition of the company's culture, which would then spread throughout the rest of the organization.

Culture Management. In 1984, Stewart Page, and Ron Harrison, and Cathrine Forest Harrison (a senior vice president), began to focus on the management of TPU's culture. Importantly, they realized that culture *can* be managed; it isn't just "there."

One of their first tasks was to define what TPU's culture was. They began with an informal culture survey distributed to a sample of employees at TPU. The survey asked respondents, who remained anonymous, a series of questions about their satisfaction with various aspects of their jobs and with the company in general. It attempted to get them to answer the underlying question "What do you see as the company's personality?" The information obtained was analyzed to determine what employees thought the current culture was. Interviews were then conducted with selected middle managers, asking them for their perceptions of the company's culture.

Stewart, Ron, Cathy, and other members of upper management now needed to decide what the definition of TPU's culture should be. They also needed to find ways to communicate the elements of this culture.

The firm also established a corporate communications department to articulate, design, and reinforce elements of the new culture. This department, headed by Mary Ryan, reported to Cathy Forest Harrison.

Another important ingredient in the process of cultural change and management at Tempo Products involved the formal and informal influence of Cathy Forest Harrison. As senior vice-president in the firm, she was responsible for one of the major functional areas of the firm. She was also, however, a co-owner of the firm and a member of its board of directors.

Cathy's role in Tempo Products' development to a stage IV company and in the redesign and management of its corporate culture was both direct as well as subtle. As a member of the board of directors, she had a senior management perspective of what was happening in the company, but she also had the ability to think about the firm in a very different way than either Ron or Stewart, both of whom were also board members. Ron was the classic entrepreneur. His skills have already been described, and he was the one who contributed the brilliant strategic vision to create the company. Stewart was the day-to-day administrator. One of his primary skills was problem solving. He was emotionally and intellectually prepared to make the difficult decisions involving people and resource allocation required at this stage of the firm's development. But successful development to stage IV also required a third type of thinking skills, the ability to think holistically about this organization and its developmental processes. Although both Stewart and Ron certainly possessed this third kind of skill to a considerable extent, in my judgment, of the three, Cathy Forest Harrison had the greatest talent for this type of thinking.

Based on her own analysis of the transformation taking place at Tempo Products, as well as on selected inputs from a consultant working with the firm, Cathy formulated her views and expressed them at board meetings thus helping to shape the corporate culture. She also championed the corporate communications department (discussed further below), and served as senior management's representative to the organization by hosting a series of working lunches to meet employees, answer their questions about the firm's future direction, and, by her very presence, communicate the company's interest in people and their concerns. She was also a major player in the decision-making process involving all of the other aspects of the organizational development program described above, including the new corporate structure, the management development program, and strategic planning.

The New TPU Culture and Its Implementation

The programs initiated in the years between 1980 and 1984 are only the beginning of TPU's attempt to redefine its culture. This process can take a number of years, and the culture will grow and change as the company does. TPU's management, however, is beginning to exercise a greater degree of control over where the company's culture is going.

This section considers how the elements of the "professional" culture at TPU have evolved from the entrepreneurial elements described in the first section of this case study. In some instances, the new culture promotes a belief, value, or norm that reflects a cultural element on which the company was based. In other cases, where going back to traditional elements would be dysfunctional, new values, beliefs, or norms need to be created and communicated. Each element of the new culture that TPU's management is creating and the methods used to disseminate it is described in the following pages.

TPU is one family, not a collection of separate families. TPU now wants to communicate to its employees the belief in a need to pull together as a company: "We can no longer operate as a group of separate entities, concerned only with ourselves."

The adoption of this belief is symbolized, in part, by the creation of the operating committee. This group is increasing communication between areas, although there is still some resistance to the idea that the company can pull together. Individual areas are still fearful that they will lose resources (power, people, materials) if they submit to the new culture. People also still want to remain loyal to their work groups, since they find the most support there.

TPU is attempting to reduce the resistance to whole-company loyalty by promoting companywide activities such as picnics, parties, and luncheons. These gatherings encourage individuals from different areas to talk with one another informally and thus establish lines of communication. The result, management hopes, will be that people feel comfortable phoning an acquaintance in another area to find the answer to a problem or question.

Another effort to re-unite the company has been the creation of a newsletter and a formal corporate communications department, which provides information on corporate activities and on the people who make up the company. In the biweekly newsletter, individuals are honored for company service, congratulated on promotions, and even given best wishes on birthdays and anniversaries. This publication is a symbol that TPU cares about its personnel. More important, from management's perspective, it also reduces employees' need to rely on the "grapevine" for information. There are many key performers in the company in addition to senior management. Previously, only two people in the firm received recognition. However, with the addition of the company newsletter and a new corporate awards program, others besides senior managers have begun to receive deserved recognition.

Decisions will be made at all levels in the company, and people will be held accountable for their decisions. TPU's management has recognized the need to develop effective decision-makers at all levels of the company and to eliminate the notion that upper management must never be challenged. To accomplish these goals, TPU has begun training individuals in effective decision-making techniques and encouraging them to apply these skills.

Participants in the management development program are formally taught how to make effective decisions. They also learn that certain decision-making responsibilities are theirs, not upper management's. TPU's management hopes that as program participants return to their jobs, they will pass on these skills to others through example and, wherever possible, through actual training of their subordinates.

Formalization of the strategic planning process is also helping to distribute decision-making responsibility throughout the organization. Individuals are being encouraged to participate in decisions affecting them by setting goals for themselves, for their work groups, and for the organization at large. Management also stresses that employees will now be evaluated on their success at meeting these goals. If employees do not understand or are unhappy with goals that have been set, it is their responsibility to clarify them.

A third way of promoting decision-making skills and reducing the practice of deferring decisions to upper management involves the refinement of role and responsibility descriptions. These descriptions, in many cases, force individuals at lower levels of the organization to become decision-makers because decision making is now defined as part of their jobs.

The new culture also stresses that no one is "invincible": everyone will be held accountable for decisions made, including senior management. The notion that senior management is invincible has been reduced not only by policy but also by example: certain members of senior management who were not performing their jobs well have been terminated.

"Whatever it takes, get it done with excellence." The emphasis that TPU has traditionally placed on excellence in products, people, and the company at large is to be maintained in the new culture. However, excellence in people will no longer be defined as "whatever TPU employees do." Rather, excellence will have the more functional meaning of quality work and desire to "do something extra" for the good of the company. A new bonus system has been created that supports this definition. This system rewards only those who perform above standard.

The management development program and the new strategic planning process also reinforce this revised definition of excellence. Both of these efforts stress that individuals will be held accountable for achieving the goals they have set for themselves and that rewards will be contingent on meeting these goals. Participants in the management development program are taught how to recognize and reward excellence in order to increase employee motivation.

Another change in the definition of excellence is that the company will no longer tolerate excessive expenditures. The "motto" now is "Whatever it takes to get it done with excellence in a cost-effective manner." Managers are held accountable for meeting their budgets, and the notion of "always going first class" is being eliminated.

Our company can learn from others. While TPU continues to promote the notion that it is a unique company, it now also wants employees to understand that it can learn from the experience of others. This belief has been promoted through the management development program, which is designed to meet TPU's specific needs and at the same time demonstrate techniques that have proved successful elsewhere. These techniques include a performance review system that evaluates individuals based on observed performance; a strategic planning system in which goals are set, monitored, and evaluated; and an organization design that is functional for the kind of company TPU has become.

We can no longer "play it by ear." TPU has recognized that some of its growing pains resulted from a lack of formalized management and operating systems. It is continuing its efforts to replace the "play it by ear" cultural element with one that emphasizes the planning, procedures, and policies of a professional firm.

At the individual level, the company has carefully reviewed the roles and responsibilities of its employees. It has got rid of most of its "deadwood" in the form of both nonfunctioning people and nonfunctional positions. This painful but necessary process has not only improved the "bottom line" but is also beginning to affect people in a positive sense. Now there is little ambiguity about job roles, and employees are aware that each has a valuable contribution to make to the company.

The communication problems that the company experienced at the management level have been difficult to resolve, but TPU's managers have come to view the new management development program as the first step toward improved horizontal communication. They hope that each group of program participants will develop a team spirit that will continue after they return to their individual areas, allowing them to feel comfortable in calling one another about problems. Upper management also hopes that these relationships will be maintained as the individuals are promoted to higher levels within the company.

Just as participants in the management development program can help to reintegrate areas on an informal basis, the strategic planning process, which emphasizes corporate rather than divisional planning, can help to reintegrate the company on a formal basis. Each area is now responsible for its own financial and nonfinancial goals, but these are to be formulated with consideration for other divisions, not in isolation from them. The planning department is helping to coordinate this effort so that company interests will remain of paramount concern.

Even more significant than the steps described above, was the firm's decision to improve horizontal communications through the creation of three separate product operating committees. Because of the nature of Tempo's products, the operating committee, consisting of representatives from different functional areas (production, sales, and so forth), is a highly effective tool for facilitating interdepartmental communication and decision making.

Have fun, but not all the time. The new culture stresses that conflict cannot and should not be avoided. Rather, conflict should be confronted and resolved.

The first step in this process is to help individuals admit that conflict exists. TPU employees had operated for many years in what seemed, on the surface, to be a very smooth-running and peaceful atmosphere. However, like all organizations, TPU had underlying conflicts between people and areas. Traditionally, these conflicts had been ignored. In 1982, however, when Stewart Page was made president and major changes began, a great deal of conflict came to the surface and could no longer be denied.

The culture survey, conducted in 1984, also brought conflicts to the surface. The survey itself was evidence that management believed that not everyone was "having fun" and that some problems existed. It was intended to reinforce the belief that "It's all right to criticize, to be unhappy about certain things. Let's get them out in the open so we can resolve our problems."

The next step is to train employees to confront conflict. This is being accomplished, in part, through the management development program. Participants are shown how to deal with conflict, particularly how to give and receive criticism. Again, management hopes that participants will take both these skills and the new culture that they represent back to their jobs and start them filtering both up and down throughout the organization. As Cathy Forest Harrison pointed out, conflict is not necessarily bad. Senior management has fostered a new culture of accountability, and this has led to conflict. Moreover, the increasing sophistication of the finance department has led to its ability, mandated by senior management, to ask the "hard" questions, which leads to conflict.

Do your own thing and do it well. Upper management at TPU hoped that this "do your own thing" element of the organization's culture would be positively redefined through the organization development program. The program could help redefine this value on three levels.

At the individual employee level, the new definition being promoted is "When you do your own thing, it should be congruent with the goals of the organization." To put this belief into concrete terms, the company is creating practices and policies that stress *real* excellence in performance and also emphasize that those who do not perform at the expected level will be dismissed. Management hopes that employees will come to recognize that those who strive for excellence will be rewarded, while those who do not will be forced to leave the company. Better definitions of roles and responsibilities act as guides to help employees determine what constitutes excellent performance. People will no longer be allowed to merely "wander the halls."

At the managerial level, managers are being encouraged to use leadership styles that will help the company be more effective. (Chapter Ten discusses the basic concepts and methods of increasing leadership effectiveness). TPU's senior management hopes that, through the training that participants in the management development program receive, they will gain the skills necessary to be effective delegators and decision-makers.

At the organizational level, the company is attempting to reduce the "do your own thing but stay out of my territory" element of its culture. This is being accomplished partly by the formation of the operating committee and partly by the management development program. It is hoped that the "team" feeling created among program participants will decrease the need for territoriality.

Conclusion

The events we have described for TPU are typical of those that occur as companies attempt to make the transition from stage II or III to stage IV. While every company, from its inception, possesses a culture, culture does not become a critical concern until the company reaches this transition period. At this stage of development, companies must become concerned with culture management if they are to continue to be successful. Otherwise, individual members of the company are likely to interpret cultural elements in ways that meet their needs but not those of the company.

To begin redefining the culture of a company, management must first determine what the culture is. This can be a difficult process, since members are not always able to articulate values, beliefs, and norms. It is much like asking a United States citizen what it is like to be an American. However, interviews with organization members, in which they are asked to relate stories about their lives in the company, may provide some clues. Careful thought and analysis, fed back to the organization for confirmation, refinement, or redefinition, is also important.

From the information provided by this cultural diagnosis, management can determine where it is in terms of culture. Then it can redefine the company's culture and begin communicating the new culture to employees through changes in policies and practices like those described here for TPU.

Several lessons can be learned from TPU's experience. The first is that the need to manage a firm's corporate culture is just as real and important as the need to manage cash or inventory. Culture can have significant positive or negative effects on operations and, ultimately, on the corporate "bottom line."

A second lesson is that cultural change is inevitable as an organization grows. Senior managers may think they know what the firm's culture is because they have a close association with the owner or founder, who directly communicates his or her vision to them. Unfortunately, as more and more new people enter the organization, the culture of the owner or founder is increasingly likely to become distorted because there is no longer much direct communication. The changes that occur are not necessarily malicious; they may simply arise from "noise" picked up through the process of cultural transmission.

A third lesson is that cultural change can reinforce and be reinforced by the broader process of organizational development that a firm must go through as it moves from stage II to stage III to stage IV. The culture that management wants to reinforce or introduce can be manifested in the firm's leadership style, its management development programs, and its strategic planning process. Indeed, the firm's culture *must* be consistent throughout all management systems if it is to become fully effective.

Another lesson concerns the process of cultural change. The change process must begin with an audit or assessment of what the firm's present culture is. This can be accomplished with a variety of tools, including questionnaires, interviews, and analysis of stories and internal corporate materials. Once the present culture has been identified, the organization must decide on the form of culture it desires and compare this ideal with the present situation. This comparison leads to identification of cultural gaps or desired cultural changes. The last step in bringing about cultural change is designing the strategy and action plan for introducing the desired changes.

A final lesson concerns the different kinds of management thinking required to develop an enterprise to a successful stage IV company. From our analysis of Tempo products it should be clear that organizational success at stage IV is more than merely a matter of products and markets, though they are an essential prerequisite. It is a matter of different modes of thinking as well. Classic entrepreneurial thinking is required for success at stages I and II. However, the successful transaction from stage II to stages III and IV requires two additional modes of thought: the problem-solving mode and the holistic organizational development perspective.

At Tempo Products, all three of the senior managers (Ron, Cathy, and Stewart) possessed each of these different modes of thinking to some extent. However, each of them individually also possessed a comparative advantage in at least one mode. As a management team, they possessed all of the three key ways of thinking about their company.

Cultural change can be accomplished through a variety of methods. As seen at Tempo Products, several different ingredients were used, including a formal corporate communications program, informal family-style gatherings, changes in senior management attitudes, a culture survey, the use of a committee structure to increase interdepartmental communication, and management development. It should also be noted that the successful organizational development at Tempo Products was not without its problems, and it is not yet fully completed. Moreover, although the roles of certain people are highlighted in this chapter, many other individuals played significant roles as well. Since this is a case study rather than a corporate history, I have emphasized the aspects most relevant to this chapter's theme.

As this chapter has shown, cultural change in a corporation is complex and difficult, but necessary. It is the critical developmental task involved in building a successful stage IV organization and making the last part of the transition from an entrepreneurship to a professionally managed firm.

PART III

Mastering the Tools of Professional Management

Parts One and Two of this book presented a framework for understanding and managing the transitions of an entrepreneurial organization from one stage of growth and development to the next. Part Three will focus on the basic tools for managing organizations professionally. Specifically, we will discuss some of the major elements of a firm's management systems. Management systems were described briefly in Chapter One, and their place on the pyramid of organizational development was shown in Figure 1.

An organization's management systems include (1) the planning system (including the strategic planning process), (2) the organization system (including the entity's organizational structure, its leadership practices, and its system for management development), and (3) the control system. Management systems have a critical influence on an organization's performance and profitability.

A firm's planning system includes its processes for strategic planning, operational planning, budgeting, and contingent planning. In entrepreneurial companies these processes tend to be relatively informal, while in professionally managed firms they tend to be more developed.

The strategic planning process is a critical resource or tool for managing organizational growth and development. Chapter Seven presents the basic concepts and methods of strategic planning. It also explains the role of strategic planning in making the transition from an entrepreneurship to a professionally managed firm by using the example of one organization's strategic plan. Finally, it examines an organization's requirements for strategic planning at different stages of growth.

The organizational control system is another critical component of the firm's management systems. Chapter Eight discusses organizational control and its role in making the transition to a professionally managed firm. It explains the need for control and the nature and role of an organizational control system. It also presents a model of the key components of a control system and explains how they function to motivate and control behavior. Finally, it examines organizations' need for control at different stages of growth.

Management development is another major tool for organizational development in entrepreneurial firms. As we saw in Chapter Six, the management development process can be used not only to train managers but also to shape or reshape the corporate culture. Chapter Nine examines the tools and functions of management development and presents a case study that shows how one company used the management development process in making its transition from an entrepreneurship to a professionally managed organization.

A fourth critical factor in managing and developing entrepreneurial organizations is leadership. Leadership is involved both in the day-to-day operations of firms and in their long-term organizational development. Chapter Ten deals with leadership. It presents basic concepts and research findings concerning leadership effectiveness. It also distinguishes between strategic and operational leadership: the former is concerned with the overall process of organizational development, while the latter is concerned with the day-to-day management of the firm. Chapter Ten examines the leadership styles available to managers in entrepreneurial organizations and presents the results of some research concerning the extent to which each style has been observed in such organizations. It also examines the key tasks that managers must perform if they are to be effective leaders and presents some research on the extent to which these tasks are actually performed by managers in organizations. Finally, it considers the nature of the leadership that is required at different stages of organizational growth.

Part Three, then, gives a basic description of some of the most important of the managerial concepts and tools that can help entrepreneurs successfully manage their firms' transition from one stage of growth to the next. These tools provide an essential foundation for the successful management of entrepreneurial organizations.

7

Strategic Planning

Previous chapters have provided an overview of the things an organization must do to make a successful transition from an entrepreneurship to a professionally managed organization. This chapter focuses on one of the major tools available to help senior managers make this transition: strategic planning.

The strategic planning process is one of the managerial systems that an organization must develop if it desires to function effectively. Strategic planning plays a dual role. It is not only an important tool for managing organizations; it is also part of the process through which organizations make the transition from one stage of growth to the next.

Strategic planning is one of the major tools by which management can create a shared vision of what a company wants to become. In other words, the strategic planning process can help to shape the corporate culture. The very act of instituting such a process, when one was not used in the past, signals to the organization's members that things are changing. It warns that planning must now become a way of life and that the firm has embarked on a program to professionalize itself. Strategic planning can also provide a sense of direction for a company and its employees as well as specific goals to motivate and guide behavior.

The Nature of Strategic Planning

In its broadest sense, strategic planning involves deciding about the future direction of an organization and the organizational capabilities that will be needed to achieve the organization's goals. It involves analyzing the organization's environment to assess future opportunities and threats, formulating objectives and specific goals to be achieved, and developing action plans to attain them. An effective strategic plan must deal not only with a company's markets and external business opportunities but also with the internal organizational capabilities required for future growth.

This chapter provides a framework to help managers understand the strategic planning process as well as a step-by-step approach to strategic planning in organizations. We will first introduce and define the basic concepts of strategic planning and then describe the seven steps involved in developing a strategic plan.

The Strategic Planning Process

The strategic planning process consists of five key phases, as shown in Figure 6: (1) the environmental scan, (2) the organizational assessment (or audit), (3) the business plan, (4) the budget, and (5) the management review.

Phase I: The Environmental Scan

As seen in Figure 6, the first two steps constitute an "environmental scan." This is an attempt to assess the future external business environment in which the organization (business or not-for-profit) expects to operate. The environmental scan must include three things: (1) a market analysis for opportunities, (2) an analysis of competition, and (3) an analysis of environmental trends. Let us now discuss each of these things in more detail.

Market Analysis. The first step in the environmental scan is to assess the organization's future opportunities. This, in turn, involves analyzing and defining the nature of the firm's business. Management must answer the question: What business are we in? Some organizations fail or at least do not prosper because they do not really understand the nature of their business. For example, during the nineteenth century and the early part of the present

**Figure 6. Flow Diagram of the Five Key Phases in the
Strategic Planning Process.**

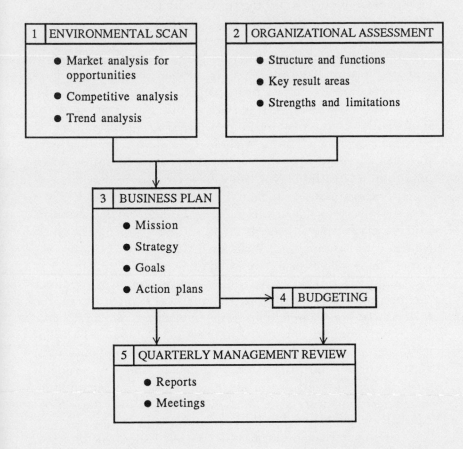

century, the railroads were successful and powerful. However, they viewed the answer to the question "What business are we in?" as obvious: "We are in the railroad business." Unfortunately for them, the "obvious" answer was not correct. They ought to have viewed themselves as being in the *transportation* business—the business of transporting people and goods. By defining their business as being railroads, they completely missed the significance of the development of air transportation, which ultimately eroded their strength.

Similarly, the Curtis Publishing Company was a great success during the early part of this century. Cyrus Curtis, a great entrepreneur, built a publishing empire with major properties such as the *Saturday Evening Post* and *The Ladies' Home Journal.* Unfortunately, Curtis Publishing Company eventually failed because it had defined its business as "the publishing business." It failed to realize that in consumer media, advertising follows consumers, and one of its principal revenue streams was from advertisers. The managers of Curtis did not appreciate the implications of the new medium, television, and its impact on advertising revenues. Thus they chose to purchase a printing plant to vertically integrate the firm's operations, turning down opportunities to acquire NBC and CBS—a disastrous decision.

An organization that is trying to decide what business it is in needs to understand what its markets are and what the customers in those markets need. It needs to answer the major questions: (1) Who are our customers? (2) What are their needs? (3) How do they acquire our products or services? and (4) What do they consider to be of value in a product or service? By focusing on these questions, the organization can define its business's purpose in the marketplace. For example, a magazine publishing company such as Curtis or Time Inc. must recognize that it serves two related but distinct groups of customers: subscribers, who read its publications, and advertisers, who wish to reach particular groups of people in order to market their own products or services. An organization must understand the needs of all its different segments of customers, especially when those needs differ significantly.

After analyzing the markets in which it desires to do business, the firm must define the products and services it will provide to satisfy the market's needs. We examined this process in Chapter Four.

Competition Analysis. The next step in an environmental scan is to assess the competition. What is the strength of our company relative to that of our competition? Does our company have a present or potential market niche? What distinguishes us from our competition? A well-thought-out and objective assessment of an organization's capabilities and those of its competition is an essential prerequisite to competitive success.

Trend Analysis. The final step in the environmental scan is to survey the larger economic, social, political, legal, and cultural environment for emerging trends that may affect the firm in the future. The organization needs to try to answer such questions as: What will our industry be like in five years? What emerging trends in demographics, workforce values, the economic and political environment, technology, and so on might affect our organization? What potential opportunities and threats are implicit in those trends? What actions can or must we take to deal with them.

Phase II: The Organizational Assessment

The second phase of the strategic planning process is to conduct an organizational assessment of the firm's capabilities. The organizational assessment focuses on each of the six key organizational development areas in the pyramid of organizational development, described in Chapter One: markets, products, resources, operational systems, management systems, and corporate culture.

The organizational assessment may be done in several ways. It may involve a self-assessment of limitations in each area. It may also involve the use of questionnaires to be completed by a sample of people in the organization or by all its personnel. Some firms use independent consultants to perform an organizational assessment; the consultants interview personnel and analyze operational data. This process, also called an "organizational audit," is described further in Chapter Eleven.

Phase III: The Business Plan

The third phase of the strategic planning process involves preparing a business plan. A business plan is a written statement of the future direction of an enterprise based on the environmental scan and the organizational assessment.

A business plan consists of five basic components: (1) the mission of the organization, (2) key result areas for planning, (3) objectives in each result area, (4) goals for each objective, and (5) action plans to attain them. Thus a business plan is simply a written document that specifies a business's mission, key result areas, objectives and goals, and action plans.

These five components of the business plan are shown schematically in Figure 7, and each component is described below.

Mission. A mission statement is a broad statement of what an organization or subunit wants to achieve during a planning period. It provides an overall sense of direction for decisions and actions. For example, a mission statement for Industrial Abrasives, Inc., an industrial abrasive distributor, for a five-year planning period might be:

> To develop into the leading full-service distributor of industrial abrasives in the western United States by 19X8.

A mission statement for a medium-sized residential real estate firm might read:

> To develop into a full-service residential real estate company, providing services throughout the northern part of the state. In order to achieve this mission, we must add to our present service capabilities in guaranteed sales, condo conversion, tract sales, investment counseling, and primary mortgages.

This statement, in addition to giving a broad description of what the firm wants to achieve, specifies the principal service components that the firm must have in order to accomplish its mission.

A more abstract type of mission statement is this one, developed by a large national certified public accounting (CPA) firm:

> Our mission is to develop a profitable, professional international accounting firm with a dynamic environment that will retain and motivate outstanding people who will provide high-quality services to business, government, and not-for-profit clients.

Figure 7. Elements of the Business Plan.

1. Mission   Broad statement of what the organization wants
                    to achieve during the planning period

2. Key result areas Performance areas that are critical to achieving
                     the organization's mission

3. Objectives   What the organization wants to achieve in the
                    long run in each key result area

4. Goals   Specific things that the organization seeks
                    to attain by a specified time

5. Action plans   Activities that must be performed to achieve
                    a specific goal

Mission statements can be developed not only for an organization as a whole but for specific subunits as well. For example, the mission statement for the personnel department of a bank with assets in excess of $1 billion was as follows:

The mission of the personnel department is to assist management with the attainment of its goals and objectives by:

1.   developing the capability to identify and meet
     the human resource needs of the bank, and
2.   developing the capability to help our people
     resource utilize their skills to the optimum.

Key Result Areas. Key result areas are the areas of an
organization's operation in which performance has a critical impact
on the achievement of the overall mission. Unsatisfactory
performance in a key result area will inhibit the organization from
achieving its mission.

Specific key result areas vary from organization to organization, and each firm must identify the ones that are relevant to its
mission. In the industrial abrasives firm cited earlier, for example,
the five key result areas were (1) profitability, (2) financial planning,
(3) management and organizational development, (4) physical plant
and equipment, and (5) marketing. The residential real estate firm
defined two broad key result areas, financial and nonfinancial. The
financial result area was further broken down into two major
dimensions: (1) company profitability and (2) profit contribution by
departments of the firm. The nonfinancial result area had five key
result dimensions: (1) company integration, (2) services offered, (3)
personnel development, (4) administration of the firm, and (5)
research.

The key result areas for a particular department, division, or
other subunit of a firm may differ from those of the overall
organization. For example, the key result areas for the personnel
department of the bank were:

1.   recruitment and selection of staff
2.   compensation and benefits administration
3.   availability of personnel data to meet management information
     needs
4.   turnover control
5.   advice on personnel matters to management and employees
6.   knowledge of EEO, ERISA, OSHA, and other regulations
7.   communication
8.   training
9.   personnel research

Objectives and Goals. Objectives are things that an organization or subunit wants to achieve in the long run in each key result area. An objective is a relatively general statement of what is to be achieved in an area. Goals, by contrast, are specific, measurable things that the organization wants to attain by a specified time in order to achieve its objectives.

For example, an objective for a medium-sized manufacturer of electronic components might be "to increase our annual sales volume," while a specific goal might be: "Increase sales volume from current level of $15 million in 19X5 to $18 million in 19X6." Similarly, an objective in the area of facilities and equipment might be "to increase our capability for inventory storage," while a specific goal might be "to relocate our midwest branch by 19X6 to a new site capable of handling 150 percent more inventory than existing facilities." In the area of profit, an objective might be "to earn a satisfactory return on investment." A specific goal might be "to earn a minimum of 18 percent ROI before taxes in each operating division."

Both objectives and goals are necessary. Objectives should not change very frequently during a planning period, while goals are subject to frequent change. For example, the objective of a marketing department for a large, Fortune 500 manufacturer of electronic equipment is to develop marketing programs for new products. A goal for 19X5 is "to plan a campaign to introduce electronic toys into the market for the winter season."

Action Plans. Action plans specify the particular activities or steps that must be performed to achieve a goal. Although action plans are not necessary for all goals, they are useful for achieving relatively complex projects or tasks.

Phase IV: Budgeting

Once the overall strategy of a business has been developed, the next step is budgeting. Budgeting involves translating an overall business plan into financial terms. The budget then constitutes a performance standard against which actual performance can be assessed.

Phase V: Management Review

The final, but very important, phase of the strategic planning process is management review, the process by which management evaluates organizational performance. This phase is also a part of the control process discussed in Chapter Eight.

I recommend quarterly management review meetings to focus on the strategic planning process. At these meetings, managers should present their results. Where actual results differ from plans, managers should explain the reasons for the differences. The use of quarterly meetings helps to reinforce the idea that strategic planning is a way of life in a company.

The specific steps in developing a plan are summarized in Figure 8, which shows that the development of a formal plan is a seven-step process, beginning from the analysis and definition of a firm's business. For example, the first two steps shown in Figure 8 are part of the environmental scan phase, while step 4.0 is part of the organizational assessment phase as well as part of the development of a business plan as such (phase III). Thus the framework is presented as a conceptual overview of a very complex, iterative process.

Metro Realty: Development of a Plan

To illustrate the process and output of an organizational plan, let us examine the planning process at Metro Realty, the medium-sized residential real estate company described in Chapter Five. The fact that Metro Realty is already familiar to you should make it easier to visualize the role of strategic planning in a firm's transition process. We will show how Metro followed the seven steps shown in Figure 8.

Define Nature of Business. At present, Metro Realty is in the process of developing toward a full-service residential real estate business. In the long run, the company may seek to become a full-service firm in the commercial as well as the residential market.

Assess Future Business Situation. As part of its annual planning process, Metro Realty identified alternative concepts of its business to guide its operations, provide direction for corporate

Figure 8. Flow Diagram of Steps in the Planning Process.

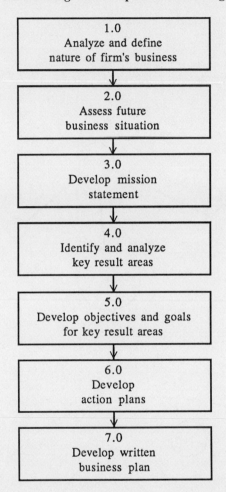

efforts, and identify or help create a market niche or competitive difference for the company. Metro Realty's alternative concepts of its business are shown in Figure 9 and described below.

Specialist in Residential Real Estate Brokerage. This concept of its business (part A in Figure 9) sees Metro Realty specializing in residential real estate brokerage with minimal support from other areas, which operate independently. This is the firm's present strategy. Following this concept, the company would add more

Figure 9. Metro Realty: Alternative Concepts of Business.

A. Specialist in residential real estate brokerage
   1. More offices
   2. Mortgages
   3. Leasing/property management
   4. Special projects

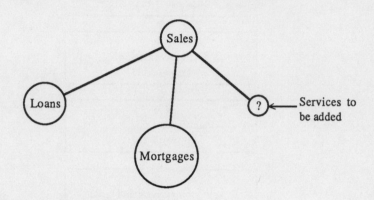

B. Full-service residential real estate firm

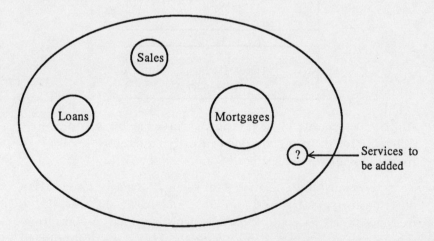

C. Full-service real estate firm

brokerage offices and maintain other functional areas at their present levels.

Full-Service Residential Real Estate Firm. This concept (B) would mean becoming capable of serving *all* of a client's residential real estate needs. It would involve identifying the full set of services required in residential real estate and building the capability of supplying those services.

Concept B, in contrast to Concept A, views loans, mortgages, relocation, leasing and other areas as integral parts of Metro Realty, not merely as adjuncts. Under this concept the development of capabilities in these areas would be an important part of Metro's objectives. An analysis of Metro Realty's major competitors indicates that all but two are moving toward becoming full-service residential real estate firms.

Full-Service Real Estate Firm. This concept (C) would extend Metro Realty's services to commercial as well as residential real estate. At present, two of Metro's major competitors have developed in this direction. Although Metro's management feels that in the long run the company should consider developing toward this type of business, revenues at the present time are not sufficient to allow adoption of this concept.

In order to choose among these concepts, Metro's annual review and planning meeting analyzed the answers to a number of questions such as those shown in Table 9. On the basis of this analysis, management decided that for the next five years Metro Realty should develop toward becoming a full-service residential real estate firm.

Develop Mission Statement. The planning meeting decided that the mission of Metro Realty was to develop into a full-service residential real estate company, providing services throughout the northern part of the state. A further aspect of Metro's mission was to become the leading residential real estate firm in its geographical area.

Identify Key Result Areas. In order to become a full-service residential real estate company, Metro Realty needed to add to its present services capability in the following areas: marketing,

Table 9. Planning Steps and Related Questions.

Step Number	Planning Steps	Related Questions

1.	Analyze and define nature of firm's business	1.1 What is the nature of our business?
		  1.1.1 Services
		  1.1.2 Markets and customers
		  1.1.3 Competition
		
		1.2 What is the firm's market niche and competitive advantage?
		  1.2.1 Do we have a special niche in the market?
		  1.2.2 What distinguishes us from our competition?

2.	Assess future business situation	2.1 What will our industry be like in five years?
		  2.1.1 Trends
		  2.1.2 Opportunities
		  2.1.3 Threats

3.	Develop mission statement	3.1 What do we want to be like or to become in five years?
4.	Identify and analyze key result areas	4.1 What must the firm do during the next five years to achieve its mission? 4.2 What are the key result areas of the business? 4.3 What are our current strengths and limitations in each key result area?
5.	Develop objectives, goals, and targets for key result areas	5.1 What are our objectives in each key result area? 5.2 What are our goals and targets in each key result area?
6.	Develop action plans for implementing objectives, goals, and targets	6.1 What are our priorities for developing programs in various key result areas? 6.2 Who is responsible for developing programs in each key result area? 6.3 What steps must be taken to achieve objectives, goals, and targets in each key result area?
7.	Develop written business plan	

guaranteed sales, condo conversion, tract sales, investment counseling and sales, and primary mortgages. Other key result areas identified by Metro Realty were profit, profit contribution, corporate integration, personnel development, and administration. As we can see, the firm identified six key result areas. These included nonfinancial as well as financial aspects of the firm's performance.

Develop Objectives and Goals. In order to work toward the corporate mission of becoming the leading full-service residential real estate firm in the area, Metro Realty defined both financial and nonfinancial objectives and goals for the period 1981–1985, as follows:

Objectives

Financial Objectives
- *Profit*—To develop profitability to a satisfactory level by 1983, through revenue increases and cost control.
- *Profit Contribution*—To develop the company so that there is a balanced profit contribution from each department.

Nonfinancial Objectives
- *Corporate Integration*—To achieve the integration of all parts of Metro Realty so that it functions as a single system rather than as a set of separate entities.
- *Services*—To review new and existing services in order to evaluate each and recommend addition, deletion, or expansion.
- *Personnel Development*—To provide education and training programs for management, sales associates, and salaried administrative personnel.
- *Administration*—To increase administrative efficiency by improvement of the management reporting system, adoption of a planning system, and development of a control system, including incentive compensation and performance appraisal.
- *Research*—To develop the capability to do research on important aspects of the business.

Goals

Financial Goals
- *Profit*—To reach profit in 1983–1985 of 10 percent (minimum), 15 percent (most likely), or 20 percent (ideal) of gross revenue, after all costs have been considered.
- *Revenue*—To base revenue on 8 percent inflation plus 1–2 percent "real" growth.
- *Costs*—To establish a standard figure for costs per employee, both direct and indirect, with the minimum being $750, most likely being $850, and maximum being $1,000.
- *Profit Contribution*—To spread the contribution of each department. Within the sales department, to redistribute the percentages of revenue contributed by different regions.

Nonfinancial Goals
- *Company Integration*—To expand and develop the relocation department in order to increase the number of referrals and integrate the department with the rest of the company.
- *Services*—To evaluate the possibility of new services in the areas of guaranteed sales, condominium conversion, tract and subdivision sales, primary mortgages, and investment and counseling.
- *Personnel Development*—To develop the following programs:
  1. A management development and training program for present members of management and management candidates that will improve the quality of management as well as providing a necessary pool of future managers
  2. An indoctrination program of six full days for all new sales associates (presently provided by the realty class)
  3. On-the-job training for the salaried administrative group to instruct them in their duties and roles in the organization
- *Administration*—To increase efficiency by the following means:
  1. Development of the capability to provide accurate and timely accounting reports; analysis of all current reporting systems to decide whether they should be continued, discontinued, or expanded

2. Completion of the implementation of the annual planning cycle, including development of a written annual corporate planning guide
3. Development and implementation of a revised incentive compensation system for all managers
4. Development and implementation of a performance appraisal and counseling system for all managers

- *Research*—To initiate research projects on the following topics:
1. Competitive niche
2. Growth
3. Franchises
4. Need for a marketing department or position

Develop an Action Plan. The next step in the planning process is to develop action plans. It is not necessary to develop action plans for all goals. Only those goals that are sufficiently complex require action plans. For example, at Metro Realty an action plan would be required for a management development and training program. Figure 10 presents an action plan for Metro Realty's 1985 management development program. It shows what tasks must be accomplished, who is responsible, and when these tasks are to be started and completed.

Develop a Written Business Plan. The next step is to prepare a written business plan. A written business plan, such as the one illustrated for Metro Realty, also facilitates the control process, as discussed in Chapter Eight.

It ought to be noted that the strategic planning process is a dynamic, ongoing process. A strategic plan is simply a snapshot of the firm's future direction at a single point in time. The plan ought to be updated annually, and strategic planning ought to become a way of life rather than a one-time exercise.

Ongoing Functions of Strategic Planning

Planning is a key component of a firm's management control system. It specifies what the organization seeks to accomplish.

Figure 10. Action Plan for Metro Realty's Management
Development Program.

Action Plan No. _1_

Key Result Area _Personnel Development_

Specific Objective _To provide continuing training for branch managers_

Specific Goal _To increase branch managers' skills in time management, delegation, and leadership_

Date Program Development Begins _March 1985_   Estimated Completion Date _June 1985_

Program Coordination Responsibility _K. Morgan_   Plan Prepared by _K. Morgan, Training Manager_

Plan Reviewed by _W. Rossien, Sales Manager_   Authorized by _T. Davis, President_

Tasks	Responsibility	Hours		Date Start		Date Completed	
		Plan	Actual	Plan	Actual	Plan	Actual
1. Prepare program budget	W. Rossien	3		3/1		3/1	
2. Search for program design consultant	K. Morgan	8		3/5		3/15	
3. Review consultant proposal	Rossien & Morgan	4		3/20		3/30	
4. Authorize contract	Morgan Consultant						
5. Develop program materials	Consultant	40		4/1		4/30	
6. Plan logistics	K. Morgan	2+		4/1		4/15	
7. Distribute materials	K. Morgan	2		5/10		5/10	
8. Conduct program	Consultant	16		6/12		6/13	
9.							
10.							

Stating the organization's mission or general direction provides a focus for its efforts. This in itself is a form of organizational control. The more specific statement of key result areas, objectives, and goals increases the degree and effectiveness of the control. A written business plan, such as the one illustrated for Metro Realty, facilitates the planning aspect of the control process by providing criteria against which performance can be measured and evaluated.

Strategic Planning at Different Stages of Organizational Growth

Previous sections of this chapter have presented the basic concepts and methods of strategic planning for entrepreneurial organizations. They have also illustrated the strategic planning process in the context of an example company. This section discusses how strategic planning should differ at each of the four stages of organizational growth.

Stage I. During stage I, strategic planning will probably be a very informal, even intuitive process done mostly or entirely by the entrepreneur. Our research has suggested that very few entrepreneurs do formal strategic planning in the sense described in this chapter.

As we saw in Chapter Four, new entrepreneurial ventures arise mostly from personal—sometimes almost accidental—insights. For example, the idea for Domino's Pizza grew out of a university student's personal need for income. Hot Rock, Inc., was born during an informal discussion at Logan Airport about business opportunities that might be developed to meet the requirements of a course in entrepreneurship.

Many times the entrepreneur is consciously or unconsciously following an informal strategic planning process at this stage. The entrepreneur often knows a particular business or industry, such as advertising, printing, publishing, ship repair, garment manufacturing, electronics, landscaping, insurance, or financial planning. Steeped in this knowledge, he or she perceives some market opportunity that is either not currently being served or not being served very well. For example, Tom Monaghan, who founded Domino's Pizza, perceived that there might be a market for high-quality delivered pizza. Similarly, another entrepreneur perceived that there was a market for budget-priced blouses among teenagers and as a result created a business with more than $80 million in annual revenues. Her concept was that the blouse ought to be priced at what a teenager could earn during one evening of baby-sitting. Another entrepreneur who became interested in computers as a hobby found that there was a market for assistance to new buyers of personal computers who were not adept at setting up the machines and making them function. The large vendors, such as IBM and Apple, simply did not bother with this service. Still another entrepreneur, a university professor of accounting who had been successful with his own real estate investments, perceived the market for a financial planning and counseling firm aimed at relatively affluent investors.

Stage II. During stage II, the informal strategic planning process of an entrepreneurial company may begin to change in certain ways. The rapid growth of the organization places considerable demands on the entrepreneur's time and energy, and his or her focus is increasingly on day-to-day operations. This leaves less time and, most important, less emotional energy to do the strategic planning required for the future development of the company. Entrepreneurs in charge of stage II companies often work sixteen hours or more per day simply handling short-term problems and trying to keep up with the momentum of business. The entrepreneur may thus become a "one-minute decision maker," not by choice but by necessity. Unfortunately, the failure to do strategic planning is itself a kind of strategic plan, for the company that does not plan its future has implicitly chosen to allow the future to happen to the organization.

At stage II a company does not need a very formal planning system, but it does need some strategic planning. Since the entrepreneur is likely to be more absorbed in other activities than was the case at stage I, it becomes necessary to substitute a system for what was initially a personal activity.

In essence, a formal strategic planning process is analogous to a "zone defense" in sports. If, for example, a college basketball team has a seven-foot center, the team is likely to have a comparative advantage in rebounding. If the team's center is only six feet six, the team is likely to be at a disadvantage in rebounding, but it may be able to compensate for this by using a zone defense. The zone defense is essentially a system in which people are positioned to perform certain tasks; in this example, they will be placed where they are most likely to give the defensive team a comparative advantage at rebounding. In effect, a seven-foot center is a one-person zone defense.

Similarly, if an organization has an entrepreneur who is brilliant at explicit or intuitive strategic planning, it may not need a formal strategic planning process. However, this presumes that the entrepreneur has the time and energy to perform strategic planning. When this ceases to be the case, the company must use a formal strategic planning process as a kind of zone defense to ensure that some strategic planning is accomplished.

During stage II, a company's strategic planning process can be reasonably simple. In a company with between $1 and $10 million in annual revenues, the process may consist merely of a one- or two-day meeting devoted to developing a corporate strategic plan, followed by departmental meetings to develop plans for each functional area in support of the overall corporate plan.

Every company, even a relatively small one, ought to be able to devote one week a year to strategic planning at stage II. If this modest amount of time and effort is not spent, there is an increasing chance that external events that may profoundly affect the company will go either unnoticed or without response.

Stage III. By the time an organization reaches stage III, it needs to establish a formal process of strategic planning. This is the professionalizing stage of organizational development, and strategic planning is one of the key management systems of a professional firm.

From approximately $10 million to $25 million in annual revenues, the major focus can be on the overall corporate strategic planning process, with departmental or functional plans done more informally. By the time an organization has reached $25 million in annual revenues, however, it needs a more extensive strategic planning process. The corporate plan should be accompanied by formal departmental plans, and the overall amount of planning time and effort should increase.

By the time a company reaches a size of $50 to $100 million in annual revenues, the strategic planning process ought to be well in place. It should be beginning to be "a way of life" in the company. Generally speaking, a minimum of two to three years will be needed to institutionalize a strategic planning process in firms of this size. The first year will simply involve the process of learning the planning system's mechanics. During the second and third years, people should increase their planning skills.

Stage IV. By the time a company has reached stage IV, the planning process ought to be well institutionalized. Strategic planning ought to be a topic in the company's management development programs.

During stage IV there can be a wide variety of refinements to the strategic planning process. At this point, for example, the company will have the resources to do more extensive market research analyses and environmental scanning studies.

A Final Note: Consultants and Strategic Planning Departments

A final issue involved in strategic planning concerns the role of external consultants and internal corporate planning departments in the planning process. The strategic plan ought to be based upon line management's decisions rather than those of consultants or a planning department. Unless the plan is "owned" by line managers, it will tend to be ignored. Consultants or planning departments can, however, play a significant role as facilitators of the planning process. They can help to plan the overall process and serve as catalysts to its completion.

An internal planning department can serve as the source of market research and other competitive information. It can also aid in the logistical aspects of the planning process. External consultants can perform these facilitative roles, too. Moreover, because of their experience with other organizations, they can provide an independent, relatively objective perspective and raise questions that can be very useful for a company. For example, this simple inquiry can be a catalyst for a fresh look at some practice: "Other companies seem to be doing it this way. What is the rationale for your company doing it that way?"

Summary

This chapter has examined the nature of strategic planning for entrepreneurial organizations. It has presented a framework of the strategic planning process, described the components of a business plan, and presented a step-by-step approach for developing a written business plan. The chapter has also illustrated the steps in developing a strategic business plan, using an example of a company. Finally, the chapter has discussed how strategic planning should differ at each of the four stages of organizational growth. This framework ought to be useful to entrepreneurial companies in designing or revising their own strategic planning process.

8

Organizational Control Systems

All organizations, no matter what their stage of development, require some form of control system. When the organization is very small, the entrepreneur can control what is happening through day-to-day involvement and observation alone. The required coordination and the information needed for decisions will appear almost by osmosis. The owner will have a good "feel" for what is happening, what the problems are, and what needs to be done; and this will be enough.

As the enterprise increases in size and gains additional people, however, the entrepreneur's ability to maintain control over all aspects of its operations will begin to decrease. The organization will begin to experience growing pains related to ineffective control systems. For example, people either deny responsibility for tasks or do everything themselves because there are no clearly defined roles and responsibilities. A company can find that its profits are low even when sales are increasing because it has no way of knowing where it is financially; this comes about when the company has not developed formal performance monitoring systems. A firm may experience a high degree of duplication of effort and decreasing productivity because of poor coordination between people and departments. All these problems suggest that one of the critical challenges facing entrepreneurs in rapidly growing companies is the need to be able to control what is happening.

Companies hire people, give them specific jobs and responsibilities, and expect them to perform well and achieve the enterprise's goals. However, the managers of successful organizations know that this is not enough. They realize that in order to be reasonably certain that the company's objectives will be achieved, they must have some way of trying to influence or channel people's behavior. In short, an organizational control system is required.

Organizations use a variety of methods to gain control over people's behavior including personal supervision, job descriptions, rules, budgets, and performance appraisal systems. These methods are all part of the organizational control system.

As we explained in Chapter Four, a formalized control system is necessary to make the successful transition to a professionally managed firm. This chapter describes the use of organizational control as a managerial tool to help in making this transition.

The Nature of Organizational Control

The term *control* can be used in a variety of ways. For our purposes it is defined as the process of influencing the behavior of members of an organization. An organizational control system may be defined as a set of mechanisms designed to increase the probability that people will behave in ways that lead to the attainment of organizational goals. This definition brings out three important aspects of organizational control: (1) it is aimed at the achievement of goals, (2) it is probabilistic, and (3) it focuses on the behavior of people.

Goal Orientation. The ultimate objective of organizational control is to try to motivate or influence people to achieve organizational goals. Its intent is not to control people's behavior in predefined ways but to influence them to make decisions and take actions that are likely to be consistent with the organization's goals.

Ideally, the objective of the control system is to increase the congruence between the goals of organizational members (individuals and groups) and the organization as a whole. This is important, because individuals will be most motivated to work toward the goals of the organization if, by so doing, they are also able to satisfy their own goals. It should be pointed out, however, that while there is usually some degree of correspondence between the goals of organization members and those of the organization as a whole, total goal congruence is rarely attained.

Probabilistic Orientation. The process of organizational control is probabilistic rather than deterministic. This means that there is no guarantee that all people will behave in ways consistent with organizational objectives all the time. Rather, there is a specified probability or likelihood that such behavior will occur.

Behavioral Orientation. Organizational control is focused on the behavior of people as members of an enterprise. Control systems are intended to motivate all employees to behave in ways consistent with organizational goals, but different aspects of a control system may be directed at different organizational levels or groups of people. A performance appraisal system, for example, may be concerned with control of individual behavior, while a budgetary control system may be more concerned with subunit (departmental or divisional) behavior.

Functions of Control Systems

In order to motivate people to behave in ways consistent with organizational goals, control systems must serve three functions. First, they must be able to influence people's decisions and actions in an appropriate direction. As we have seen, without an effective control system, people are likely to make decisions and act in ways that fulfill their own personal needs and goals but not necessarily those of the organization. At Tempo Products Unlimited, for example, employees and departments "did their own thing" without considering the needs of the company as a whole. This resulted in a number of people and departments who did nothing at all or who, consciously or unconsciously, worked at odds with the goals of the company. It also resulted in duplication of effort between departments, which contributed to increased costs.

Control systems must also coordinate the efforts of diverse parts of an organization. Even when people are trying to act in the best interests of a company, they may find themselves working at cross purposes. As we saw in the case of Custom Printing, lack of coordination can result in duplication of effort, production delays, and other inefficiencies. At Custom Printing, there were a large number of rush orders because coordination between sales and production was poor. When orders were rushed, many had to be redone because of mistakes in production, which resulted in unanticipated delays for customers and increased costs for the company. Lack of coordination between shipping and production contributed to shipping delays and resulting customer dissatisfaction.

The third function of control systems is to provide information about the results of operations and people's performance. This information allows the organization to evaluate results and make corrective changes as required. Even if individuals, groups, and the organization have common interests, problems may occur that require correction. At Custom Printing, for example, few people knew whether they had met their goals because there was no way to monitor their performance. This resulted in a number of unmet goals for which there were no repercussions. People could not be held accountable, since they had no way of knowing what their performance was. Similarly, managers at Metro Realty could not be held accountable for failing to meet their budgets because the information necessary to monitor financial goals was not available. When profits began to decline, the company was unable to take corrective action because it did not have adequate information on income and expenses. At Tempo Products, a lack of adequate information contributed to poor performance and ineffective operations. Employees did not know how to improve their performance because managers were reluctant or unable to provide both positive and negative feedback. The result was that, even when individuals were performing poorly, they continued to operate in the same fashion as they had before the evaluation.

Elements of Formal Organizational Control Systems

An organizational control system is a system designed to control some sort of organizational activity, such as sales, production, or engineering. More formally, it may be viewed as a set of mechanisms designed to increase the likelihood or probability that people will behave in ways that help to achieve organizational goals.

The organizational control system focuses on some aspect of human behavior that has to do with attainment of organizational objectives. Such behavior may include acquisition, allocation, utilization, development, conservation, or disposition of organizational resources. We refer to these activities or functions as the operational or behavioral system.

The four basic components of a system of organizational control are: (1) objectives for the performance of the activity or function; (2) goals for performance on each specified objective of the activity or function; (3) a method of measurement for monitoring the performance of members of the organization; and (4) a method of administering rewards to motivate and reinforce performance (the evaluation/reward process). The relationships among these four components is depicted in Figure 11. We will now describe each of these components further.

Objectives. As described in Chapter Seven, objectives are the things an organization wants to achieve in a given result area. For purposes of this discussion, it is useful to think of two types of objectives, ultimate and instrumental. Ultimate objectives are broader and tend to be related to the primary mission of the organization. They might be such things as earning a satisfactory return on the assets used in the business, developing a new market for a product line, or expanding the scope of the business to meet a competitive threat. For example, Kawasaki Motors has as one of its corporate objectives an increase in market share of 1 percent each year for the next five years.

Instrumental objectives (subobjectives) are the means by which the ultimate objectives are achieved. For example, the firm that has as its ultimate objective the development of a new market for a product line would have instrumental objectives dealing with desired sales of that product for a given period, production objectives for the product, and marketing campaigns and costs. Some instrumental objectives are stated in monetary terms through budgets, while others are part of the broader planning process.

Figure 11. Model of Organizational Control System.

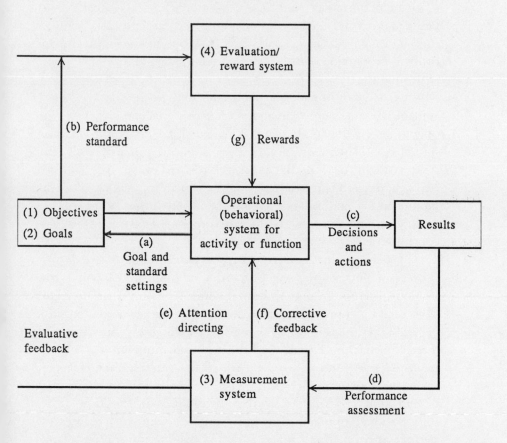

Both ultimate and instrumental objectives help to direct or channel the efforts of people in an organization. They are both means to achieve desired ends and a form of ends in themselves.

Goals. As described in Chapter Seven, goals are specific, measurable, and time dated. A goal states what performance ought to be in order to achieve a given objective. The objective of a salesperson may be to generate revenue for the firm, while the goal for the revenue may be last month's (or last year's) sales plus 5 percent. Goals may be based on management judgment, expectations, or historical data.

Goals may be used to establish desired performance levels, to motivate performance, and to serve as a benchmark against which performance can be assessed. For example, "standard costs" can be used in a manufacturing plant as a goal to motivate employees to control production costs and also as a way to evaluate their performance.

Goals are intended to facilitate both *ex ante* and *ex post* control. *Ex ante* control is motivation of performance before the operation or behavioral system is executed. Goals in this area are intended to bring about desired performance levels in people. *Ex post* control uses goals as standards in evaluating actual performance and as a basis for rewards, which, in turn, reinforce or modify future performance. Goals, then, play a significant role in evaluation and rewards, the fourth component of organizational control systems.

Measurement and Reporting System. Measurement is the process of representing the properties or qualities of objects in numerical terms. In organizational control systems, measurement has a dual function. One purpose is to provide information that can be used for evaluating performance and making corrections in goal-directed behavior. This is the informational function of measurement. The accounting system, with its measures of financial and managerial performance, is a part of the overall measurement system that contributes to the informational function. The informational function also draws on nonfinancial measures of performance such as market share, production indices, and measures of product quality.

Measurement also plays another role in control systems. The very act of measuring something has an effect on people's behavior because people tend to pay more attention to the aspects of jobs or goals that are measured. This aspect of measurement may be termed the "process function." It is related to Marshall McLuhan's notion that the medium is the message.* The medium of measurement is itself a stimulus.

* M. McLuhan, *Understanding Media: The Extensions of Man* (New York: McGraw-Hill, 1964).

An effective control system ought to measure all major goals because of the process function of measurement; otherwise, some goals may be ignored. For example, if a store uses an incentive pay plan that compensates employees on the basis of sales volume as a performance measure, those employees will tend to compete for sales and ignore unmeasured functions such as stock work.

Reporting or feedback is also an important part of an organizational control system. A variety of reports, ranging from financial statements to cost reports and performance reports, provides information about the results of operations to management and others.

Performance Evaluation and Reward System. The final component of an organizational control system is the evaluation and reward system, which facilitates both *ex ante* and *ex post* control. Evaluation determines how well individuals and groups have done in meeting organizational goals. Evaluative reports generated by the measurement system, containing such items as net income, budgets compared to actual, and return on investment, generally are used in performance evaluation. Through evaluation, the organization decides how individuals and groups will be rewarded.

Rewards are desirable outcomes of behavior required by organizations. Organizations offer a wide variety of rewards, ranging from monetary items such as compensation or bonuses to recognition and promotion. Rewards can be extrinsic or intrinsic. When people perform tasks because work is interesting, their rewards are intrinsic. When people perform tasks because of the rewards they expect to receive from others, such as praise or pay, the rewards are extrinsic.

Whatever the nature of rewards, they should reinforce positive performance and modify negative performance. Further, the rewards must be *seen* as being linked to desired behavior in order to be effective as motivators.

Sometimes organizations fail to offer rewards that motivate people to perform desired behavior, or they offer rewards for one type of behavior while actually trying to motivate another—"the folly of rewarding A, while hoping for B."* For example, a business manager may be rewarded only for not exceeding his budget, even though the firm hopes that he will also pay attention to personnel development.

Rewards can be useful in motivating employees before behavior occurs because of the expectation of rewards in the future. Once good performance occurs, rewards reinforce the behavior and lead to the greater probability of it happening again. Behavior that is not followed by a reward is less likely to happen in the future.

All the components of the control system affect the operational or behavioral system for an activity. As shown in Figure 11, the control system's process of objective and goal setting initially channels effort. Once set, the objectives and goals become performance standards that function in both *ex ante* and *ex post* control. In their *ex ante* function they serve as inputs to motivate behavior in the operational system, while in their *ex post* function they are inputs to the evaluation and reward subsystem. Measurement directs attention toward measured dimensions of goals and provides corrective and evaluative feedback. Organizational rewards serve both *ex ante* and *ex post* control functions. *Ex ante,* they are a source of arousing motivation toward organizational goals. *Ex post,* they reinforce or extinguish behavior.

Design and Evaluation of Control Systems

Effectiveness. The effectiveness of a control system is measured by the extent to which it increases the probability that people will behave in ways that lead to the attainment of organizational objectives. If a control system sometimes leads to goal congruence and sometimes to goal conflict, it is ineffective, or at least less effective than might be desired.

To be effective, a control system must identify all behaviors or goals that are required by the organization. If the system does not identify all relevant goals and seek to control them, people may simply channel their efforts toward some desired but uncontrolled

* S. Kerr, "On the Folly of Rewarding A, While Hoping for B," *Academy of Management Journal,* December 1975, pp. 769–783.

behavior. In addition, in order to be effective, the control system must actually lead to the behavior it is intended to (or purports to) produce. For example, a control system may be intended to motivate people towards achieving both a budgeted profit and personnel development. If it produces this effect, it is said to be "behaviorally valid." If it leads to behavior that is in conflict with these goals, it is "behaviorally invalid." In general, a control system cannot be expected to lead to behavior that is totally consistent with what is desired, but it must have some degree of behavioral validity if it is to be effective.

A control system's effectiveness also depends on the extent to which it repeatedly produces the same behavior, whether this behavior is intended or not. This quality is called the control system's "behavioral reliability." A control system may have a high degree of behavioral reliability but lead consistently to unintended behavior, or a system may lead to intended behavior but do so irregularly.

Lack of Production of Dysfunctional Behavior. When a control system is ineffective, dysfunctional behavior can result. There are two types of dysfunctional behavior: goal displacement and measurementship.

Goal displacement is a lack of goal congruence created by motivation to achieve some goals sought by the organization at the expense of other intended goals. Goal displacement may be caused by several things, including suboptimization, selective attention to goals, and inversion of means and ends. Suboptimization occurs when the performance of an organizational subunit is optimized at the expense of the organization as a whole. It is caused by factoring overall organizational goals into subgoals and holding individuals and units responsible for those subgoals. It is a common problem and is difficult to avoid in large, complex organizations.

Selective attention to organizational goals is closely related to suboptimization. It occurs when certain goals of the organization are pursued selectively, while other goals receive less attention or are ignored. A third type of goal displacement is caused by the inversion of means and ends. This occurs when a control system tries to motivate attention to certain instrumental goals, which become ends in themselves because of rewards and thereby prevent achievement of other goals.

Measurementship involves a lack of goal congruence created by motivation to "look good" in terms of the measures used in control systems, even though no real benefit is produced for the organization. It involves manipulating the measures used by a control system—playing "the numbers game." There are two primary types of measurementship: smoothing and falsification.

Smoothing is an attempt to time activities in a way that produces the appearance of similar measures in different time periods. For example, a manager may wish to smooth the calculated net income number in two adjacent periods. If profit is expected to be unusually high during the first period, this figure can be smoothed by incurring expenditures then that otherwise would have been made in the second period in the prior year.

Falsification is the reporting of invalid data about what is occurring in an organization in order to make a person or an activity look good in the management system. A large toy company, for example, was recently charged with manipulating sales by intentionally accounting for certain transactions incorrectly in order to show good earnings for the stock market.

Problems related to dysfunctional behavior point to the importance of designing and implementing effective control systems at each stage of organizational development.

Control Systems at Different Stages of Organizational Growth

No single control system is ideal for every organization. Each organization is different and requires a different type of system. The major factor that determines the amount of control a given organization requires is the company's stage of growth.

Stage I. Even the smallest organizations need some type of control system, but at stage I, control typically is relatively informal. Usually the entrepreneur can exercise control during stage I simply through his or her day-to-day interaction with people in the organization. By the very fact of constantly being there, the entrepreneur is able to observe what is happening and be on top of almost everything. At this stage, the entrepreneur still knows all the company's employees. He or she is able to observe what most of them are doing and suggest modifications when necessary.

Even in this informal stage, however, the basic functions of control need to be exercised. The organization should have a basic budgetary system and an accounting system. The latter can be a manual system at stage I, although a computer-based system is preferable. (Several existing software packages are appropriate for stage I companies.) At stage I a company can get by with a relatively informal performance appraisal system, but there ought to be some regular appraisal process.

Stage II. As soon as a firm reaches stage II, its control needs increase dramatically. The entrepreneur no longer has the time to handle control singlehandedly, nor can he or she personally interact with all of the growing number of employees. There is increased need for the kind of coordination that only a formal system can bring. If the entrepreneur fails to recognize the need for a more formal control system, the company is likely to experience difficulties.

During stage II, a company ought to be beginning to develop a formal planning system that includes the basic elements described in Chapter Seven. It also needs a more formal control system to help it carry out its plan. It will most likely need to change its basic accounting system to some kind of "responsibility accounting system," which provides information not only on overall financial performance but on product line profitability and business segment profitability as well.

In stage II, the evaluation and reward component of the control system must also be developed further. Job descriptions specifying responsibilities are required. Some sort of "management by objectives" approach ought to be introduced, accompanied by a formal performance appraisal system. The firm's compensation program also ought to become more systematic and include an incentive component that is linked to performance. Failure to make these changes during stage II may lead to the feeling that the organization is "out of control."

Stage III. By the time a company has grown to stage III, it requires more sophisticated and powerful methods of control. This is the stage at which the company must develop a formal control system along with other components of its management systems.

As we have noted, planning at stage III needs to be brought down to the level of individual products or profit centers. Similarly, the company's budgeting system needs to be brought down to the level of individual products or profit centers. Similarly, the company's budgeting system needs to be brought down to the level of individual departments and products.

The company's accounting information system will typically need to be reconceptualized to provide a greater amount of information for management control. By the time a firm reaches stage III, it ought to have a well-developed responsibility accounting system. It should also have a well-developed set of management reports dealing with the nonaccounting information that is required to monitor the business.

By this stage, performance appraisal linked to management by objectives also ought to be a way of life. A formal performance appraisal system should be in place, and management development programs should have taught the firm's managers how to use it effectively.

If management did not lay the foundation for these systems during stage II, they will be more difficult and costly to develop during stage III. If the firm still has not put the systems into place by the time it reaches the later phase of stage II, it is likely to experience serious growing pains. These may be masked temporarily by continually rising sales if the firm is in a favorable market. Unfortunately, when the market ultimately turns, the company may find itself facing a "scissors effect" of simultaneously reduced revenue and increased costs. This can prove fatal.

Stage IV. By the time a firm reaches stage IV, its basic organizational control system should be in place. Most of the changes to be made at this stage are (or at least ought to be) merely refinements.

The planning system will become more sophisticated. Relatedly, the budgeting process may be refined to include features such as flexible budgeting (budgeting based on different assumptions about the economy and related level of business). The accounting information system ought to be able to generate accurate, timely, comparative data.

A performance appraisal oriented to performance against plan ought to be a part of the firm's corporate culture. Evaluation meetings ought to be regularly scheduled, and employees ought to expect that deviations from standard will require factual explanations.

In brief, by the time a company reaches stage IV, its organizational control system ought to be well developed, functioning smoothly, and in place as an integral part of its overall corporate culture.

Conclusion

When an organization passes the size at which the entrepreneur can personally function as its control system, the owner will increasingly be stretched thin, and with the addition of other people and managers, the need for coordination will grow. There will also be a need for information about problems being encountered in various aspects of operations, including receivables, inventories (if any), and sales. Thus there will be a growing need for formal controls to supplement the personal involvement of the entrepreneur.

Unfortunately, organizations do not have to be very large before it becomes extremely difficult, if not impossible, for the entrepreneur to perform all functions of the control system. In fact, by the time a company reaches $1 million in annual revenue, it becomes highly unlikely that the entrepreneur alone will be able to exercise effective control. This chapter has described the basic concepts that the entrepreneurial firm can use to develop the type of control system required at its particular stage of organizational development.

9

⊗⊗⊗

Management Development

Management development is another major tool available to the senior management of an entrepreneurial organization that is trying to make the transition to a professionally managed company. It can help to meet one of the greatest ongoing needs of rapidly growing entrepreneurships, the need for managerial talent. Many CEOs of such firms are familiar with the cry "We just don't have enough good managers!"

Management development can provide people with the skills they need to effectively manage a firm. But sophisticated companies such as IBM, Hewlett-Packard, and Motorola recognize that management development is more than a tool for training people in new skills. It is also a tool for educating managers in the company's corporate culture—its values, beliefs, and norms.

This chapter begins by discussing the general role of management development in organizational development and transitions. It then examines this topic further by describing how one company, Knapp Communications Corporation (KCC), used its management development program to assist it in making the transition to a professionally managed organization.

The Nature of Management Development

Management development is the process of building the present and potential performance capabilities of an organization's

This chapter was coauthored by H. Stephen Cranston, president of Knapp Communications Corporation.

managers. It can focus upon managerial skills, attitudes, and experiences as well as the manager's perception of his or her role.

As has been noted, one of the critical problems in growing entrepreneurial organizations is the lack of sufficient good managers. To repair this lack, a firm can hire experienced managers from outside the organization, develop them from within, or do both. Most successful firms use both external recruitment and internal development.

Management development is just as real an investment as the investment in plant and equipment. It is an investment in the human capital of an organization—the skills, knowledge, and experience of people. It is an investment in the infrastructure of an organization.

Some of the country's most successful and progressive organizations invest heavily in management development. At IBM, for example, management development is a way of life. It is woven into the fabric of the organization.

Within thirty days of being appointed a manager at IBM, an individual must begin a program of basic management training. This program teaches the fundamental skills needed to perform effectively as a first-line supervisor. IBM also requires that each manager have a minimum of forty hours of additional management development training each year. At IBM, management development is viewed as an ongoing process, and the firm has made a significant commitment of resources to it.

Many successful smaller entrepreneurial organizations follow a similar strategy. The entrepreneurs of those organizations recognize that one of the critical factors in their companies' ability to continue to grow successfully will be the presence of sufficient managerial talent. As the owner of one firm that had grown in about seven years to more than $100 million in revenues stated: "We have plenty of product and expansion ideas, and I can borrow money for expansion from a bank; but my critical need is for people who will be capable of managing what we plan to become."

Although management development can play a positive role in building managers, it is not a panacea. It cannot be expected to turn people into "managerial wonders" overnight. The development of managers takes time. Consequently, it is useful to regard management development as a process of "building managers."

Functions of Management Development

Management development has several functions, all of which are especially relevant in organizations making transitions from one stage of growth to the next. The most obvious is to enhance the skills of the firm's managers. Management development can also be used to (1) help define or redefine the corporate culture, (2) help promote the style of leadership that the organization desires, and (3) serve as a reward to or recognition of good managers. Let us discuss each of these uses further.

Shaping the Corporate Culture. One of the most powerful uses of management development programs is to help articulate and communicate the corporate culture. Programs may communicate culture by various means, such as using example cases to describe "how we do things here at General Products Corporation" and identifying "heroes" who personify corporate values and serve as models to be emulated.

Promoting Leadership Style. Another major function of management development programs is to communicate the leadership style that is acceptable in the organization. Some firms, such as IBM, promote a version of "contingency theory," which postulates that the appropriate style of leadership depends upon the nature of the situation. (This approach is described in Chapter Ten.) Other organizations promote a single style of leadership. For example, Motorola promotes participative leadership.

Rewarding and Recognizing Managers. Some organizations use participation in management development programs as a reward. A reward program may be held at an off-site location, such as a resort, and the entire event will be designed to be a pleasurable experience. Closely related to the reward concept is the use by some organizations of selection for management development as a form of corporate recognition. It is intended as a signal to both the individual and the rest of the firm that the person is valued.

Knapp Communications Corporation: Management Development in the Transition to Professional Management

To illustrate the role of management development in making the transition from an entrepreneurship to a professionally managed organization, we will examine the way it was used by Knapp Communications Corporation (KCC). Under the leadership of C. T. Knapp, founder and chairman, and H. S. Cranston, president, KCC used management development as part of an overall strategy to professionalize the firm. Management development helped the firm achieve certain aspects of development at both stages III and IV of corporate growth.

Corporate Background. In the mid-1960s, Cleon ("Bud") Knapp acquired *Architectural Digest* magazine from the estate of his maternal grandfather. *Architectural Digest,* the cornerstone of what was to become Knapp Communications Corporation, was at that time a small-circulation Southern California magazine of interior design. For several years, Knapp worked to create a new product from the magazine he had purchased, and it ultimately became the leading magazine of interior design in the world.

Beginning in 1975, KCC experienced extraordinarily rapid growth. It acquired a second magazine, *Bon Appetit.* Revenues increased from $2 million in 1975 to $100 million in 1982. Personnel increased from about 30 in 1975 to more than 450 by 1983.

This period of growth occurred because KCC had learned to do some fundamental things very well. The firm's founder, Bud Knapp, has the classic skills required for entrepreneurial success: the ability to identify a market need and niche, the ability to produce a product appropriate for that niche, the willingness to risk, and the ability to attract talented people to assist him in building the enterprise. Specifically, the firm has learned how to identify a magazine market need, redesign an existing magazine to gear it to the market's requirements, and produce and sell the "new" publication.

During KCC's process of growth, Bud Knapp was well aware of the need to make the transition to professional management. By 1983 the company had already taken steps to develop its management systems and capabilities. Specifically, the firm had initiated a strategic planning process, engaged in a corporate reorganization, and begun a series of management development activities for middle-level executives.

Growing Pains. A key step in the process of professionalizing KCC focused on management development as a way of solving certain problems that had come to plague the company. One problem was a lack of managerial talent. As KCC grew, it was forced to promote to managerial jobs many people who were talented "doers" and technicians who had not been trained as managers. Such people quickly found themselves stretched beyond the limits of their experience and formal training. The firm grew so fast that it was always on the treadmill of hiring new people and promoting others before they were prepared to assume managerial responsibilities. These people were managers in title only.

A related problem was that since KCC merely continued to add people as it grew rather than reconceptualizing its organizational structure, it was in essence an overgrown version of a small company. As one person stated, "We were a $5 million company that happened to have $75 million in sales."

Adding to these difficulties, employees at KCC had fallen into the "Superman syndrome." (As noted throughout this book, many companies suffer from this same problem.) The company's founder, Bud Knapp, was viewed as a genius; even articles in the popular press credited him with the "Midas touch." People were used to kicking problems upstairs to Bud. He was an authority without being authoritarian, and many people correctly assumed that his decisions would be better than theirs. Unfortunately, the firm had passed the size where one person could deal with everything—but neither the management systems nor the managerial personnel were yet in place to substitute for "Superman," who found even his considerable abilities stretched to the limit. The firm had simply been so busy keeping up with its rapid growth that it had had no opportunity to "grow" the systems and managers it now required.

Another set of problems created by the firm's success involved its culture. One manifestation of this was in employees' financial expectations. Since the firm was successful, Bud Knapp had been generous with compensation and bonuses. Some people therefore began to expect compensation and bonuses as entitlements rather than as rewards for effort. Others expected to be rewarded lavishly for merely average performance. People began to regard bonuses as a "base" part of their compensation.

The firm's success also led to a kind of organizational hubris. Many people began to believe that because KCC produced excellent products, it must also be excellent in everything else it did, including personnel management, administration, and so on. This was an admirable performance standard. Unfortunately, however, it was viewed not as a goal to be attained but as a reality. Relatedly, the firm had begun to become ethnocentric; that is, many people had begun to think in terms of "the Knapp way" of doing things. The firm had done things its own way throughout history, and that had worked out very well. This led to the belief that "we are different from and better than everyone else in publishing." Although this type of self-confidence can often lead to a self-fulfilling prophecy of success, it can also have the negative side effect of causing people not to seek or to ignore new ideas from outside the organization.

Another dimension of the cultural problem was attenuation of KCC's original culture. As you have seen, this often occurs in organizations that have reached growth stage IV. Basically, as more and more people entered the firm, they found increasing trouble in understanding the corporate culture because it could no longer be effectively communicated through face-to-face interaction, the means of dissemination on which KCC had traditionally relied.

Objectives of KCC's Management Development Program

Although KCC recognized the need for a formal program of management development to facilitate the growth of its future executives, there was some dissatisfaction with prior efforts in this area. The firm had offered a variety of management development sessions for its present and potential managers, but there was no overall concept of these programs' goals. The management development activities had been presented by a variety of different instructors from both inside and outside the company, and the quality of their programs varied widely. The programs offered had been open to all who wished to attend, which led to significant differences in the knowledge and abilities of those enrolled in any particular program at the same time. Finally, the programs offered were geared to the development of managerial skills, but they failed to deal with other equally important but more subtle aspects of management development.

Because of these problems, KCC decided to experiment with a different approach to management development. It arranged for an overall program of management development that was geared to meet a broad range of management development needs, including (1) development of basic management tools and skills both in people who had already been promoted to management positions and in people who might soon be promoted, (2) creation of a cadre of young first-line supervisors who would be able to move into middle management positions when needed, and (3) reinventing reestablishing the firm's value system among the newer members of management, who in turn would transmit it to their staffs. We will now look more carefully at some specific objectives of KCC's management development program.

Develop a Cadre of Future Managers. One of the major objectives of KCC's program was to develop a cadre of future managers who would be able to move into middle management positions as the firm continued to grow. The idea was not only to develop individual managers but to try to create a company team analogous to the one that had existed during the firm's initial stage of development. This peer group, senior management hoped, would grow together as the firm continued to develop. The plan was to bring this group together in the program, enable them to interact, and hope that this would lead to future informal interactions that could help to overcome the "separate island syndrome," the condition in which each functional area of a company operates so totally independently that effective coordination does not occur.

Develop a Managerial Viewpoint. Another major objective of the program was to help people begin to think and act like managers rather than technicians or doers. Although many individuals occupied managerial positions, they had not yet begun to think or behave like leaders. The goals in this area were to teach people what a manager was, that a manager was a leader, what the differences between a manager and a doer were, and what each individual would have to do to make the transition from a "doer" psychology to a managerial and leadership psychology.

Develop Managerial Tools and Skills. Another objective was, of course, to help participants develop their skills as managers and to learn about the tools available to managers. KCC conducted a needs assessment to identify the skills that should be taught. This assessment involved both interviews with potential course candidates and discussions with selected senior managers in the firm. The firm's president, H. S. Cranston, also suggested skill areas he felt were important, including understanding of the management role, people management skills (including motivation and communication), and accounting skills for nonfinancial managers.

Reestablish the Firm's Value System. Bud Knapp recognized that the firm's basic values had not been accurately transmitted to newer employees. He also understood that the informal mechanism through which this cultural transmission occurred in the past would no longer function, because of the firm's size. For this reason, one of the explicit objectives of the management development program became reestablishment of the firm's value system. In meeting this objective, the most important part of the program was to be the establishment of the idea that the values of a business enterprise are the enterprise's most important aspects. Some specific values to be emphasized concerned standards of excellence.

A basic cultural assumption that management hoped to reestablish through the program was that the only form of control that is effective or worthwhile is that resulting from self-motivation. As stated by Cranston, "The belief that one *must* do one's best can only be a personal obligation and cannot be imposed. If demonstrated, however, it can be emulated by others, provided it is based upon a value system that goes beyond the desire for material fulfillment."

Another implicit goal of the management development program was to cause people to realize the futility of searching for panaceas or easy answers. Management wanted to avoid the "current management guru system," in which everyone blindly studies "the word" in the latest best-selling book on management techniques.

Initiate a Cascade Effect. KCC's management hoped that the new program would initiate a "cascade effect" in which the participants in the program would go back to their posts and motivate changes that would cascade down through the organization as the trained people were promoted and managed more and more employees. The group was intended to motivate changes upward in the organization as well, in that the very existence of a cadre of trained junior managers could motivate others to develop their skills and "buy into" the value system being demonstrated by the class graduates.

Nature of the Program

KCC's management development program was intended to be of high quality, rigorous, and demanding. Designed by a management development firm consisting of experienced university educators, it was of a quality and difficulty comparable to MBA-level courses at a leading university. No explicit rewards were offered either as inducements to enter the program or as recognition of its successful completion. Participants in the course would receive a "Certificate of Completion" and a token momento but no bonuses or salary increases. The primary rewards were intrinsic: the satisfaction of meeting demanding standards—of being able to say, "I did it!"—and of the experience itself.

Unlike most management development efforts, the program developed at KCC was designed as an integrated course. The course was to be conducted over a nine-week period. It would include case histories, films, role-play simulations, and exercises as well as selected readings and lectures. A binder of materials was prepared for each participant. Each participant had to complete three written assignments during the course. Participants needed a grade of "B" or better to pass the course.

Some of the example cases used in the program drew on existing materials. However, five case histories were specially written for the context of Knapp Communications Corporation. These new case histories were intended to increase the meaningfulness of the concepts and tools presented by showing their relevance to day-to-day problems faced by managers in that firm and to increase the familiarity of each participant with other areas of the corporation. Role plays, also specially designed for KCC, were intended to increase the meaningfulness of program materials by means of both experiential learning and contextual relevance.

Impact of the Program

In order to assess the extent to which KCC's management development program was able to achieve its objectives, we administered a questionnaire at both the beginning and the end of the course. This questionnaire was designed to assess the overall extent to which an individual had made the transition from a "doer," or performing, orientation to a managerial orientation, based on four specific dimensions that have been hypothesized to be key elements of the required transition: (1) the person's concept of his or her role, (2) the types of skills possessed, (3) the psychology of managing one's self, and (4) the psychology of managing others. Responses to this questionnaire showed that the program had made a significant difference in the students' thinking.*

During the period in which the course was conducted, the class evolved, as hoped for, from an *ad hoc* group to a traditioned group. A considerable degree of "we-feeling" developed, and the class even set up its own unofficial graduation. In part, this was an effect of the well-recognized "common fate syndrome," the affection that develops among individuals who have shared a demanding experience.

Management Development at Different Stages of Organizational Growth

This section examines the different needs for management development that companies have at the four stages of organizational growth.

* For a discussion of the statistical effects of this program on the participants, see H. S. Cranston and E. G. Flamholtz, "The Role of Management Development in Making the Transition from Entrepreneurship to a Professionally Managed Firm," *Journal of Management Development*, forthcoming.

Stage I. At the earliest stage of growth, most organizations do not have formal management development programs for their people. Management development takes place, if at all, through on-the-job training. Although some management development would be desirable for companies in stage I, the cost of establishing an in-house training program is usually prohibitive at this point.

In spite of this, stage I is a good time to begin establishing the organization's cultural attitude toward management development. The firm can hold an annual one-day in-house seminar on a management development topic, or it can support attendance at public seminars. It can purchase and distribute management books to its employees or purchase management magazines for circulation. Employees can also be encouraged to participate in continuing education programs or even acquire MBAs. Most significantly, the founding entrepreneur can serve as a role model and stress, through word and behavior, that management development is important in his or her firm.

Stage II. During the early part of stage II, a firm can continue the same approach to management development that was recommended for stage I. After the firm has reached approximately $5 million in annual revenues, however, it is probably ready for and can afford some form of in-house management development program as well.

The principle management development goal for a stage II company is to ensure that all its managers understand at least the basic skills of management. At this point most people will be first-line supervisors; that is, they will be managing one level of personnel rather than managing other managers. Such people require training in the fundamentals of supervision, including people management skills (motivation, communication, performance appraisal, conflict management), as well as in basic skills in work planning and organization and personal time management. They should understand the fundamentals of delegation and the need to begin to think and act like a manager rather than a "doer."

The principal advantage of using an in-house program to provide this training is that the program can be tailored precisely to the firm's people and their needs. A firm may find it useful to have an outside professional management educator help in designing and implementing the program. The firm can typically find such assistance at a local university.

Stage III. By the time a firm has reached stage III, it ought to be in the process of developing an in-house program of management development. At this stage, the key organizational development issue is professionalizing the firm and its management systems.

To accomplish the transition to professional management, the organization must change the way it thinks about itself and the way it operates. The founder/entrepreneur will no longer be able to fully manage all aspects of operations personally. He or she will have to use other managers as surrogates. This does not—or should not—mean that the entrepreneur simply uses these managers as extra "arms and legs" to perform specific tasks; rather, there should be a real delegation of authority. The entrepreneur must learn to trust managerial subordinates to perform their responsibilities well. This, in turn, means that these people will have to think like entrepreneurs or businesspeople rather than simply as functional specialists. To accomplish this change, some form of management development is typically required. The management development program at Metro Realty, described in Chapter Five, is one good example.

Assuming that an organization has already laid the foundation for management development in stage II by providing a basic supervisory skills program for its people, a major management development goal for a stage III company will be to reinforce these basic skills. Such skills are not simply learned once and then fully retained. People get into and out of habits, and skills must be reinforced. For example, one function of the five-year driving renewal test is simply to motivate people to read the test booklet again and remind themselves of what they ought to be doing. Although most people probably consider it a pain to go through the driving renewal test, it is likely to make them remember long-forgotten parts of the "rules of the road." Doing so reinforces the way they ought to be driving.

The primary goal of stage III management development, however, is to provide the advanced skills of managerial leadership, strategic planning, departmental organization, and control systems required by people who are or will be managing other managers. The skill of strategic planning was described in Chapter Seven, and effective leadership is discussed in Chapter Ten.

Stage IV. After a firm has reached stage IV, it will have a greater degree of discretionary resources. Wise officers planning for the successful long-term development of their entreprises will then want to invest considerably in building human assets through management development programs. They will realize that their firms are competing not merely in products and technology but in people as well.

A stage IV company definitely ought to have an in-house management development program. Our example of Knapp Communications Corporation presented a model of the type of thinking that should underlie a stage IV company's program.

A typical stage IV company will have its own human resources department and training staff. In addition, most firms supplement their in-house staff by using either outside university educators or consultants to help design and deliver management development services.

The primary goal of a stage IV management development program is to train and develop people with either a general management or a senior management perspective. The need for managers at stage IV relates to the consolidation of the enterprise as well as to preparation for future growth and development. There is a qualitative difference in the type of managerial skills and capabilities required by managers at this stage.

A stage IV organization is a very significant entity. A great deal of effort is required to manage the internal organization and the business of such a firm. To accomplish this task, managers require a holistic perspective. They need to think in terms of the pyramid of organizational development both for the care and feeding of the existing enterprise and for the development of new entrepreneurial ventures that will replicate the growth cycle that the parent company has already gone through.

Training people to think strategically and conceptually about the development of an organization requires a more sophisticated type of management development. It requires the use of case histories and exercises designed to broaden the perspectives of people who are used to thinking in more narrow terms as functional specialists. Yet it is essential if a firm is to maximize its chances to grow and develop successfully.

Summary

This chapter has presented a case study of how an entrepreneurial company can use management development to help make the transition to a professionally managed firm. The case illustrates the various functions and uses of management development in making this transition. Knapp Communications corporation used the management development program not only to increase people's skills but also to help reestablish the firm's culture, to create a cadre of managers who would serve as role models in the organization, and to promote a new style of management in the company. Although this is not the only model of using management development, it provides a powerful tool for companies in the process of moving from stage II to stage III or IV. The chapter has also examined the different levels of management required at different stages of organizational growth.

10

⬤⬤⬤

Effective Leadership

One of the most critical managerial functions in entrepreneurial organizations is leadership. Effective leadership is a prerequisite not only to successfully making the transition from one stage of a firm's development to another but to operating effectively at any stage.

Leadership can have many styles. U.S. managers have come to recognize that Japanese managers use a leadership style different from those used most often in this country. They have also begun to appreciate that there are significant differences in management style among U.S. organizations.*

The purpose of this chapter is to provide basic concepts, ideas, and research findings concerning leadership effectiveness. The framework we present is a synthesis of various schools of leadership research. A basic premise underlying our discussion is that the two key factors in effective leadership are (1) the choice of the correct leadership style for a particular situation and (2) the performance of certain key tasks of leadership.

The entrepreneurial manager needs to select a style of leadership appropriate for an organization's current stage of growth. To aid in this selection, we will examine the nature of organizational leadership and point out two different types of

*See, for example, the discussion of the difference management style can make in successful organizations in T. H. Peters and R. H. Waterman, *In Search of Excellence* (New York: Harper & Row, 1982).

I am indebted to Yvonne Randle for research and editorial assistance in the preparation of this chapter.

leadership relevant to entrepreneurial organizations: strategic leadership and operational leadership. We will then examine a variety of different leadership styles and the factors that must be considered in selecting a leadership style. We will also present some research findings relating to the nature of leadership styles found in entrepreneurial companies. After a brief discussion of leadership theories, we will describe the five key tasks an effective leader must perform. Finally, we will consider the nature of effective leadership at different stages of organizational growth.

The Nature of Leadership

Leadership is the process whereby an individual influences the behavior of people in a way that makes them more likely to achieve organizational goals. Under this definition, leadership is an ongoing process, not a set of traits that a person possesses. The process involves understanding, predicting, and controlling others' goal-directed behavior. The leader's ultimate objective is to create a goal-congruent situation—a situation in which employees can satisfy their own needs by seeking to achieve the goals of the organization. Leadership, then, like organizational control, is behaviorally oriented and goal directed.

As noted earlier, two general types of leadership are relevant to the management of entrepreneurial organizations, strategic leadership and operational leadership. Strategic leadership is the process of influencing members of an organization to plan for the long-range development of the firm in the six key areas making up the pyramid of organizational development: markets, products or services, resources, operational systems, management systems, and corporate culture. It is oriented toward the development of the organization as a whole and of the organization's ability to function in its environment. Lee Iacocca's performance at Chrysler was a fine example of strategic leadership. Operational leadership, by contrast, is the process of influencing the behavior of people to achieve operational goals. This dimension of leadership is concerned with the day-to-day functioning of the enterprise.

Both types of leadership are essential for the long-range survival and growth of an entrepreneurship, yet a single individual may not possess the ability to perform both leadership functions. For this reason, some organizations appoint both a chief executive officer (CEO), who is responsible for strategic leadership, and a chief operational officer (COO), who is responsible for operational leadership. This occurred at Tempo Products Unlimited, as we explained in Chapter Six.

Styles of Leadership

A quarter century of research has failed to confirm that there is one style of management that is best for all situations. Rather, there are a variety of styles, each of which may be effective or ineffective depending on the circumstances. This notion has been called "contingency theory" or "situational leadership."*

The following pages describe six basic styles of leadership.† These styles constitute a continuum that goes from a very directive to a very nondirective leadership style, as summarized in Figure 12.

---

* For discussions of a contingency theory see, for example, F. E. Fiedler, *A Theory of Leadership Effectiveness* (New York: McGraw-Hill, 1967). For a discussion of situational leadership, see P. Hersey and K. H. Blanchard, *Managing Organizational Behavior* (Englewood Cliffs, N.J.: Prentice-Hall, 1977), 159–186.

† The late Rensis Likert developed a classic typology of four basic leadership styles (autocratic, benevolent autocratic, consultative, and participative) in his book *New Patterns of Management* (New York: McGraw-Hill, 1961), 222–236. This typology was subsequently retitled as "Systems I–IV" in Likert's *Human Organization: Its Management and Value* (New York: McGraw-Hill, 1967), 3–12. R. Tannenbaum and W. Schmidt independently developed the concept of a continuum of leadership styles in their article "How to Choose a Leadership Pattern," *Harvard Business Review*, March–April 1958. The conceptualization in this chapter is related to both of these prior efforts. The labels for our first four styles of leadership are identical with Likert's, but the definition of behavior we use for each style differs to some degree. The other two styles we list, consensus and laissez-faire, represent somewhat different patterns from those previously conceptualized by others.

Figure 12. Continuum of Leadership Styles.

Directive		
↑	1. Autocratic	I'll tell you what we are going to do because I'm the boss.
	2. Benevolent autocratic	I'll tell you what we are going to do because it will be best for all concerned.
	3. Consultative	I'll decide, but I'll discuss it with you to get your opinions.
	4. Participative	We'll decide together, but not all votes are equal.
	5. Consensus	We'll all meet and discuss it until everyone agrees on a decision.
↓ Nondirective	6. Laissez-faire	Do whatever you want to do.

It should be pointed out that this is but one of a variety of leadership classification schemes. The major point to draw from it is that in their purest form, these styles are indeed different and may therefore be appropriate for different situations with different personnel.

The Autocratic Style. The autocratic style is a very directive style of leadership. A manager who uses this style promotes the notion that he or she has the authority to make *all* decisions and does not feel the need to explain the decisions' rationale to subordinates. This style can best be characterized by the statement "I will tell you what we're going to do because I'm the boss" or "Look, I'm head of the department; I'm being held responsible. I will tell you what we're going to do, and that's that."

The Benevolent Autocratic Style. The benevolent autocratic style is a "parental" style of leadership: the leader acts on the assumption that he or she knows what is best for the organization and the individuals involved. The degree of direction used in this style is essentially the same as in the autocratic style, but the style is more benign. A manager who uses this style will usually explain the rationale behind decisions, while an autocratic leader will not. A person adopting this style might say: "I'll tell you what we're going to do, because that will be best for all concerned." Where an autocratic leader might say, "As a condition of coming to work here, you are obliged to accept what I say," a benevolent autocrat might say, "This is what I want you to do, but I've taken your needs into account."

The Consultative Style. The third style of leadership is qualitatively different, at least to some degree, from the first two. A person adopting this style reserves the right to make the final decision but actively seeks the opinions of others concerned first. To illustrate the difference between this style and the other two, suppose a manager is presenting the organization's goals for the coming year. An individual operating with the autocratic style might say: "This is what we're going to do. These are our goals for next year." A benevolent autocrat might approach the situation with "This is what the organization needs, and here is how it will affect you." In contrast, a manager utilizing the consultative style might say: "Here is what I think our goals ought to be for the next year. What's your reaction?" This manager will still make the ultimate decision, however.

The Participative Style. Inherent in this fourth style of leadership is the idea that a decision should be made on the basis of group input. This does not mean, however, that all votes on an issue are equal. The leader still reserves the right to make the final decision, as in the consultative style.

The basic difference between the participative and consultative styles is the manner in which others' opinions are solicited and used. In the participative style, the group actually helps to develop ideas rather than just giving input on the manager's ideas. In the consultative style, the manager might come into a group and say: "Here is what I think we should do. Give me your reaction." The manager using a participative style, on the other hand, may have an idea about what the group should do but basically will say: "Here are the problems. Let's discuss them together and come up with recommendations. Then I'll make the final decision." In the latter instance, the manager might begin a meeting by expressing his or her own stance, but the group will be allowed to participate in solving the problem by making recommendations.

The Consensus Style. The consensus style represents another qualitative shift along the continuum of styles. A leader adopting this style uses the same format as one utilizing the participative style, but in this case, the leader's vote is virtually equal to all others. This leader does not reserve the right to make the final decision but rather emphasizes the importance of developing group consensus on the matter at hand. A person using the consensus leadership might say: "Let's meet, discuss the problem, and reach an agreement on its resolution. I will run the group only as a facilitator because I believe that if you all agree to something, you will be highly motivated to achieve it. I will not, therefore, exercise a high degree of authority." A group with a leader who uses this style is thus given more responsibility than in the other styles.

The Laissez-Faire Style. The most non-directive style of leadership, laissez-faire, places the responsibility for task accomplishment completely upon the subordinate(s). A leader utilizing this style essentially says: "Do whatever you want to do."

There are two versions of this style, one positive and one negative. A leader operating under the positive version promotes the notion that highly trained individuals do not need a great deal of direction. This type of leader thus gives his or her subordinates a great deal of independence. Such a leader might say, "You know what your job is. Do whatever you have to do to get it done." The more negative version of the laissez-faire style might be characterized by the statement "Do whatever you want to do. Just leave me alone." This is an "abdocratic" style, an abdication of authority and responsibility.

Leadership Styles in Entrepreneurial Organizations. Our research and consulting work has shown a wide variety of leadership styles among CEOs and other managers of entrepreneurial organizations. The most common styles, however, were the consultative and participative styles. The participative style was somewhat more common in high-technology manufacturing and service organizations, while the consultative style was more common in low-technology manufacturing. Perhaps as a reaction to the behavioral literature of the 1960s and 1970s, there seemed to be relatively few managers who used autocratic or benevolent autocratic styles.

Factors Influencing Choice of Leadership Style

It is important to understand that a manager does not have to always use the same leadership style. An individual may adopt a variety of styles, each suited for a particular situation. We have found that consideration of six key factors can help managers in entrepreneurial firms decide which style is best at a given time. The first two factors we will discuss are the most important; they probably account for 80 to 90 percent of the influence on leadership effectiveness in a given situation.

Nature of the Task. The aspect of a work task that is most important to consider is probably the degree of programmability of the task. If a task is highly programmable (that is, the optimal steps for its completion can or may be specified in advance), then a directive style of leadership is appropriate. If the task is nonprogrammable (that is, the nature of the work necessitates a great deal of variation in individual procedures), a directive style may be difficult or impossible, and a more participative or nondirective style will be required. In other words, the greater the degree of programmability of the task, the more appropriate it is for a manager to say: "This is the right way to do this task; we know it's right because we've studied it and worked out the best way to do it." Where the task is less programmable, the manager must use a more interactive or laissez-faire approach.

Nature of the People Supervised. This factor is really made up on a variety of subfactors, including people's skill and education levels, their degree of motivation, and their desire for independence on the job. This latter subfactor refers to the degree to which workers prefer to be on their own, do their jobs, and then return with results as opposed to wanting more interaction, feedback, and supervision.

Taken together, all these subfactors can be thought of as a single variable called "potential for job autonomy." The more highly educated, highly motivated, highly skilled, and in need of independence a person is, the higher his or her potential for job autonomy. Conversely, a person with low education, low task-relevant skills, and low need for independence has a low potential for job autonomy.

People with different potentials for job autonomy require managers with different leadership styles. A nondirective style (consensus or laissez-faire) will be most appropriate with workers who have a high potential for job autonomy, while a very directive style is appropriate with workers who have low job autonomy. A more intermediate style of leadership is needed when workers do not fit one or the other extreme. For example, a person who is highly motivated and working at a job that requires a high degree of nonprogrammability but is not very skilled may require a leader who adopts a style somewhere in the middle of the continuum, either consultative or participative, at least until the person becomes more experienced.

Figure 13 shows the relationship between the two factors we have just described and the six leadership styles described in the previous section. As can be seen in the figure, a high degree of programmability combined with a low potential for job autonomy would ideally require a directive style. At the other extreme, low programmability and high job autonomy, a nondirective approach would be most effective. The other two cells show intermediate conditions where an interactive approach would best fit the situation.

Supervisor's Style. If a difference exists between a supervisor's preferred leadership style and one or more subordinates' style(s), it will be difficult for the subordinate(s) to justify their own style unless the supervisor allows the use of it. A subordinate may feel a need to change his or her style to make it closer to that of the supervisor. In other words, supervisors have a tendency to consciously or unconsciously evaluate their subordinates on the basis of their own leadership styles. The manager in the superior position in such a situation may need to recognize that people can use different styles and still be effective.

Peers' and Associates' Styles. The dominant style of his or her peer group can also influence a manager's choice of leadership

Figure 13. Factors Affecting Choice of Leadership Style.

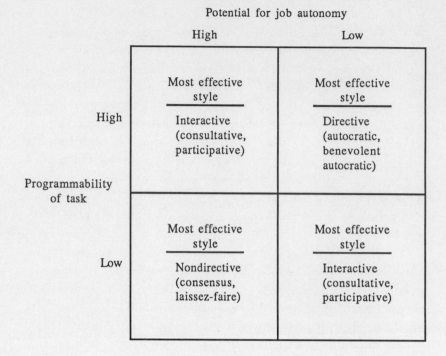

style. For example, if most managers in a particular group use a consultative style and a few use a benevolent autocratic style, the latter individuals will feel some pressure to change their style to make it more like that of the majority.

Amount of Available Decision Time. People are much more willing to accept a directive leadership style in crisis situations than in situations where nothing needs to be decided in a hurry. If someone in a roomful of people says, "I see smoke," people will not expect to be asked to form groups and discuss alternatives for action. Most individuals will probably be quite comfortable with someone's saying, "Stand up and calmly walk out the door, down the hall, and out into the street."

Nature (Culture) of the Organization. Each organization has norms concerning the type or types of leadership style(s) felt to be appropriate for its members. These norms affect all members of the organization. For example, Motorola recently autocratically decided that it would become a participatively managed organization. People were asked to change their leadership styles to become participative managers. If they could not or would not, they were explicitly or implicitly encouraged to leave. This organization essentially said, "Look: to compete effectively with the Japanese, we are going to have to be a participative organization, because the kind of people we're attracting want a say in what they're doing. Therefore, we will be participatively managed."

These, then, are the factors that affect the choice of leadership style. They can be analyzed to determine what kind of style would be more appropriate in a particular situation with particular types of personnel.

Leadership Theories

In the study of leadership, the initial emphasis was on attempting to identify the personal characteristics of effective leaders. After more than two decades of research, this approach was abandoned in the mid-1950s because a set of consistently valid and reliable predictive factors could not be identified. This does not mean that such factors absolutely do not exist; it could mean that the statistical tools used were not powerful enough to detect them. In any event, the leadership "trait" theory was abandoned, and a leadership process approach was adopted. This new approach proved to have much greater predictive value.

The leadership process approach is based on the premise that leaders can be developed. Instead of being born with certain personalities, as the trait theory suggested, this approach suggests that leaders can learn what to do to be effective. Further research was then conducted to determine what differentiates effective from ineffective leaders. Two key factors, task orientation and people orientation, were identified as being important characteristics of effective leaders.

For a time, these two factors defined two divergent schools of thought about leadership. The school of neoscientific management argued that concern for task made a leader most effective, while the "human relations school" argued that concern for people and their needs was the critical variable. However, empirical research showed that neither factor alone was sufficient to explain leadership effectiveness. Both factors appear to be important and independent dimensions of leadership. An effective leader needs to be concerned about both task performance and the nature of the people being supervised.

Key Tasks of Effective Leaders

Subsequent research has identified five specific subfactors that further define the two dimensions of effective leadership just described.* In other words, to be effective leaders, managers must perform five key tasks, which we will describe in the following pages. Each of these tasks can be effectively performed using any of the leadership styles previously defined. As we have noted, the best style to use depends on the situation.

Goal Emphasis. An effective leader emphasizes the attainment of goals through goal-setting processes, focusing upon goals, and monitoring of goals. The late Rensis Likert, an internationally noted behavioral scientist, pointed out that to be effective, a leader has to demonstrate a "contagious enthusiasm for the achievement of organization goals."

Note that in this emphasis on goals, the effective leader's style can range from autocratic to laissez-faire. An autocratic leader might simply say: "Here are our goals." At the other extreme, a laissez-faire leader might say: "Let's agree on what our goals are, then you figure out how to achieve them." At the intermediate level, a person with a participative or consultative style might say: "Here's what I think our goals should be. What do you think?"

* This conceptualization is a slight modification of the four-factor theory of leadership proposed by D. Bowers and S. Seashore in "Predicting Organizational Effectiveness with a Four-factor Theory of Leadership," *Administrative Science Quarterly*, 11, (1966): 238–263. The four factors identified by Bowers and Seashore were goal emphasis, work facilitation, interaction facilitation, and support. In this chapter we have subdivided the factor originally labeled "support" into two dimensions: (1) supportive behavior and (2) personnel development.

Interaction Facilitation. An effective leader must be able to coordinate people and facilitate effective interaction among them. An effective leader can either manage meetings or create them in a way that allows people to work together effectively and cooperatively. Someone with a directive leadership style might accomplish this by saying: "We're having a meeting. This is our agenda, and this is what we're going to accomplish." A more nondirective way to do the same thing might be to act as a facilitator at a meeting, helping to summarize what people are doing and asking nondirective questions.

Work Facilitation. The third thing an effective leader does is to help personnel achieve their goals by facilitating their work. This can be accomplished in a variety of ways, including helping to schedule a task, making suggestions about how it should be done, providing reference materials, and suggesting knowledgeable sources of information regarding task procedure. A very directive way of facilitating work might be to say: "This is the way you should be doing your job." At the other extreme, a person using a laissez-faire style might simply ask nondirective questions or suggest that people look in certain areas for help.

Supportive Behavior. A fourth task of an effective leader is to provide supportive behavior in the form of both positive and negative feedback to subordinates. Positive feedback is important, since it serves to reinforce appropriate goal-oriented behavior and thereby increase the chances that the behavior will continue to be performed. Negative feedback, in the form of expressed dissatisfaction with work and constructive criticism, tends to eliminate dysfunctional behavior.

A directive leader might express supportive behavior with "No, John. Don't do it that way. Do it this way." A person using a more nondirective style might handle a similar situation with "I'm going to have to evaluate what you do on this project. You do a self-assessment at the same time. Then, let's meet and compare notes, and we'll see where we need to go from there." An extremely nondirective approach might be to say: "You've just completed the project. I want you to review your documentation and critique it. What have you done well? What have you done poorly, and how will you better this in the future?"

Personnel Development. The effective leader helps to develop people. He or she motivates people to be concerned about their future development and to analyze their specific needs for development. As was the case with the other factors, the leadership style used to perform this task can range from directive to nondirective, depending on the personnel and the nature of the work being done. A directive approach might be to say: "I think you should go to a management training program." A nondirective approach might be to say: "What do you see as your developmental needs? I want you to think about them and to decide what you want to do to meet them."

Performance of Key Leadership Tasks in Entrepreneurial Organizations. Our research with entrepreneurial organizations has led to certain general findings. We have noted, first, that there is a consistent underemphasis on the leadership task of goal emphasis in such organizations. Perhaps because entrepreneurs are so goal oriented themselves, they may expect their subordinates to be equally goal oriented and therefore they may not perceive the need for further direction. Second, we have found a consistent tendency for the supportive behavior task to be performed in entrepreneurial firms to a somewhat greater extent than standard. The larger the firm, the more emphasis it is likely to place on this task.

Effective Leadership at Different Stages of Organizational Growth

Previous sections of this chapter have presented the basic concepts and research findings concerning leadership effectiveness that are relevant to managers in entrepreneurial organizations. This section deals with the question of how leadership should differ at various stages of organizational growth.

Stage I. During the first stage of organizational development, it is likely that the entrepreneur, either individually or together with a small team, will be responsible for all major decisions in the organization. This will include both operational and strategic decisions. It is also likely that the entrepreneur will be in the best position to make most of those decisions. He or she will have an open-ended commitment to the business, and the firm will still be small enough for the entrepreneur to be on top of almost everything. Accordingly, it is likely that the benevolent autocratic or autocratic style of leadership will be used and will be acceptable to most members of the organization.

At this stage, the entrepreneur will probably be concerned more with work facilitation and supportive behavior than with the other key leadership tasks. While the organization is relatively small, goal emphasis will occur almost by osmosis—that is, by day-to-day interaction of employees with the founder(s). Since there will be relatively few people, formal interaction facilitation also will not be necessary. People will interact in the natural course of their transactions. Similarly, personnel development will occur simply as a by-product of on-the-job training and probably will not require formal training programs.

Stage II. During stage II, it is likely that the style of leadership used in stage I will still be reasonably effective. However, emphasis will increasingly have to be placed on the performance of the five key tasks of leadership.

It is surprising how soon the clarity of goals begins to break down as organizations increase in size. An organization does not even have to exceed $1 million in annual revenues before a lack of clarity in organizational goals can arise. Thus there will be an increasing need for goal emphasis. Similarly, even with a relatively small number of people, a growing need for interaction facilitation will occur. Meetings for the purpose of communication rather than for making decisions will have to start being regularly scheduled. During this stage the entrepreneur's time will be increasingly filled, but the need for work facilitation will not diminish. Since the organization will be high on its own adrenalin, the need for positive support may not be intense, but the rapid growth of the enterprise will lead to hiring mistakes and, therefore, an increase in the need for corrective feedback (a part of support). The need for personnel development will also be increasing during this growth stage.

Stage III. The critical factor in leadership effectiveness during stage III will be the need to begin to make a transition from a directive style to a more interactive style, such as the consultative or participative style. This means that the entrepreneur must begin to give up some degree of control and learn how to delegate authority rather than merely delegate tasks. Delegation of tasks involves telling people what you want them to do, while delegation of authority means letting people be responsible for an area— letting them have a say in setting the goals to be achieved as well as in deciding how those goals are to be accomplished.

The transition in the style of leadership that must be made at this stage is complex, and many entrepreneurs never accomplish it. Their failure in this regard places their companies in jeopardy, because organizations outgrow the entrepreneurs' ability to make all decisions. (Changes in leadership style that a CEO must make during this transition are discussed further in Chapter Eleven.)

Entrepreneurs during stage III need to begin developing a trained cadre of managers to whom they can feel comfortable in delegating authority. They need to make sure that these managers know how to perform the five key leadership tasks.

Stage IV. The key leadership need in stage IV is to articulate and spread the company's culture through the organization. This means that managers must be trained to use a more participative or consultative style with their subordinates. The leader also needs to help create and disseminate a shared vision of what the company is to become. When the company was smaller, the concept of its future direction could be communicated more informally. By the time a firm reaches stage III or stage IV, however, senior management must exercise the process of strategic leadership to develop and communicate this common vision. This can be done through the strategic planning process described in Chapter Seven.

Summary

This chapter has defined leadership as a process and has presented information that should help managers make that process more effective. It identified six different leadership styles, ranging from very directive to very nondirective. It noted that there is no one most effective style; the most effective leadership style in a particular situation is determined by a variety of factors, including the nature of the task being performed and the nature of the people being supervised.

The chapter also discussed the key tasks that effective leaders perform. Effective leaders are both task oriented and people oriented. They emphasize goals, facilitate interaction and work, are supportive of personnel, and encourage personnel development.

Each manager has the potential ability to choose a leadership style to fit any situation and group of people. This ability can be improved by increased awareness of the factors that influence the choice of effective leadership style and increased development of the skills needed to accomplish the tasks that effective leaders perform.

PART IV

❧❧❧❧❧❧❧❧

Role of the Entrepreneur
in a Growing
and Changing Company

The previous sections of this book have examined the organizational issues that face companies making the transition from an entrepreneurship to a professionally managed firm. But organizations consist of people, and these people must go through personal and professional transitions in order to handle the organizational changes we have described.

Although all members of an organization are profoundly affected by its transition, no one is more influenced by the changes involved than the organization's senior management, especially the CEO or founder(s). The transitions required may lead to a great deal of organizational and personal trauma, as in the case of Apple Computer, which lost both its founders, Steven Wozniak and Steven Jobs. These men, who were responsible for the founding and development of a $2 billion organization and for the technical innovation and entrepreneurial vision that created Apple, were replaced by John Sculley, a professional manager brought in from Pepsico by Jobs himself.

Other entrepreneurs face a similar fate unless they are able to change along with their companies. Chapter Eleven deals with some of the personal, professional, and organizational transitions that the founder or CEO of an entrepreneurial organization must make if the organization is to continue to grow successfully and profitably. The issue here is not whether entrepreneurship or professional management is better. Both are valuable, but each is suitable for a different stage of organizational growth and development.

Chapter Eleven begins with an examination of the personal issues facing the CEO during organizational transitions and the alternatives available to him or her. Next, it considers the organizational issues facing the CEO and the steps that the CEO can take when faced with the need for an organizational transition. The chapter also identifies stages of growth beyond stage IV, which organizations will encounter as they grow further. Finally, Chapter Eleven offers some additional advice to CEOs concerning their role, their organization, and its management during the transition process.

11

The Transitions
CEOs Must Make
to Survive Beyond
the Entrepreneurial Stage

Most of this book has dealt with the organizational and managerial issues that arise when entrepreneurial firms make the transition from one stage of growth to another. This chapter, by contrast, is more personal. It is directed primarily to the CEO of an entrepreneurial company, because this person will have the major responsibility to direct and guide the transition process of the whole organization. However, the ideas included here should also be of interest to senior managers, corporate advisors, venture capitalists, and others who are concerned about the welfare of business enterprises.

The chapter will focus on two kinds of issues facing the CEO: (1) personal issues, such as the nature of the CEO's role, behavioral and attitudinal changes required, and changes required in managerial style during organizational transition, and (2) strategic issues involved in designing and implementing the changes required for healthy organizational development. In the latter context, we will identify some stages of growth beyond organizational maturity (stage IV).

Personal Issues

In order to understand transitions that CEOs must make as their firms grow, it is useful to first consider who they are as people and how they got to be CEOs. Unlike the CEOs of large, Fortune 500–type organizations, who are typically promoted through the ranks over a period of many years, the CEO of an entrepreneurial company is typically someone who either founded the company, was part of a founding group, or is the spouse or a child of the founder.

Characteristics of Entrepreneurs. Although there are no precise demographic and psychological profiles available, our experience has shown that CEOs of entrepreneurial companies tend to have certain things in common. About 90 percent of these people have one of three types of background: (1) a marketing background, (2) a background in some technical area, such as engineering or computers, or (3) a background in a particular industry. For example, an individual may have sold computers for a large company before deciding to start his or her own company. Alternatively, a person may have been an engineer or other technical specialist and become skilled at product development before deciding to establish a new business. Finally, someone may have worked in a particular industry such as travel, executive search, construction, real estate, or garment manufacturing.

Most CEOs of entrepreneurial firms are enthusiastic about markets and products but are not very interested in management or the "nuts and bolts" of day-to-day operations. Many of them find accounting boring. They have no more interest in their own accounting system than the typical homeowner has in the household's plumbing: they want it to work, but they do not care to understand how it works. Many tend to look at financial statements only to determine "the bottom line."

Entrepreneurs are typically above average in intelligence, willing to take risks, uncomfortable in environments in which they are told what to do, and fond of seeing things done their way. Most, but not all, do not have good listening skills. They are used to being the dominant person in business situations. Most of these CEOs have made open-ended commitments to their business, which means that business does not merely consume a great deal of their life; in most instances, their business *is* their life. The pejorative term *workaholic,* however, would be a misleading description of such people; rather, they view the business as a rather complex game. It is a source of profound personal pleasure. Above all, entrepreneurs possess a strong desire to be independent of others' ability to control their behavior. They like to feel "in control."

The Personal Control Bind. The most important of all these characteristics, from the standpoint of making organizational transitions, is the entrepreneurial CEO's desire for things to be done his or her way—the desire for control. The typical CEO of an entrepreneurial company either consciously or unconsciously values control both as an end in itself and as a means to other ends. This personal preference has most likely been reinforced in a variety of ways for a relatively long time.

During the first two stages of organizational growth, the typical attributes of an entrepreneurial CEO are beneficial and necessary for the company. Fledgling enterprises need strong direction and open-ended commitment to make everything work properly. At this time, a compulsive CEO who knows about everything that is going on and pays attention to the smallest detail will have a tremendous positive impact on operations.

Many consequences of an entrepreneurial CEO's desire for control, however, are less favorable during the later stages of a company's development. Specifically, both the CEO and the organization's staff may have become used to the idea that almost every issue, whether major or not, will be brought to the CEO's attention for decision or final approval. More insidiously, if the CEO has not been extremely careful, an entire organization inadvertently may have been built on people weaker than the CEO. In other words, the CEO may have become an unwitting bottleneck in the organization. Even though the firm has grown in size and added many managers and professional specialists, the CEO may remain the most skilled person in the company in most, if not all, areas. This means that the CEO has not been able to increase the company's capabilities beyond his or her own admittedly considerable personal skills. Such a situation puts limits on the organization's capacity to grow and develop.

The CEO's desire for personal control over everything done in the organization, which was a considerable strength during stages I and II, thus becomes a limitation or bind on the company during stage III. Some CEOs consciously want to retain control and therefore do not want to hire people who are better than they are at any particular task. Others are afraid that if they hire someone to perform a task that they cannot do themselves, they will become too dependent on that person. For example, the CEO of one service firm with $5 million in annual revenues was doing most of the company's computer programming work himself. When asked why he was spending his time in this way, he replied: "If I had someone else do it, I would be vulnerable if he left me."

Some CEOs are able to recognize their own limitations relative to their companies' changing needs. As one founder and CEO of an entrepreneurial firm stated: "I'm an entrepreneur. I'm very good at controlling things—making a decision and seeing it accomplished by sheer willpower alone, if necessary. But our company has grown beyond that style. I'm not uncomfortable with the company, but I'm not as effective." Such CEOs realize that, for the good of the firm, they need to make the transition from a manager who is used to controlling everything and being the center of all that happens to someone who is still important but is not an omnipresent, omnipotent figure.

Even when the need for it is recognized, however, this type of change can be stressful. For some CEOs, whose identities are closely bound up in their companies, it represents a threat—a potential loss of potency. Many CEOs are simply not able to give up control to any significant degree and end up strangling their organizations.

Some CEOs go through the motions of giving up some degree of control because intellectually they know that this is essential, but emotionally they cannot really bring themselves to do it. For example, one entrepreneur built an organization that achieved a billion dollars in revenues in less than one decade. Recognizing that the size of the enterprise now made it impossible for him to manage in the old way, he brought in two "heavy-weights": experienced, professional managers whom he had to pay high salaries to attract. One was a marketing manager, and the other was a finance-oriented manager who would be responsible for day-to-day operations. The entrepreneur himself moved up to chairperson. Unfortunately, he then proceeded to turn the professional managers into "managerial eunuchs." When the organization began to do poorly, he announced that he had experimented with professional managers but, reluctantly, he had to reassume personal control himself.

Alternatives for the CEO. Four basic alternatives are available to the CEO of an entrepreneurial organization who recognizes that the organization can no longer be run in the old way. They are (1) do nothing, (2) sell the business and start over, (3) move up to chairperson and bring in a professional manager to run the organization, or (4) make a systematic effort to change personal behavior to fit the needs of the company at its new stage of development. Let us look more closely at each of these alternatives.

First, the CEO can do nothing—or, rather, do "business as usual"—and hope for the best. This could be called the "ostrich strategy." The strongest argument for this course of action is that the company has been successful with its current style to date, and "if it's not broken, don't fix it." Unfortunately, corporate graveyards are littered with companies that had promising starts but, because of this strategy, did not continue to develop.

The second strategy is for the CEO to become chairperson and bring in a professional manager to run the business. This is the approach Steven Jobs tried at Apple Computer. After Apple reached a billion dollars in revenues, Jobs recruited John Sculley of Pepsico, who had the track record of a successful professional manager. The pitfall of this strategy is that if it is to be effective, the founder must give up considerable control to the new manager. The strategy also may not work out politically. It certainly didn't for Jobs, who has now left the chairmanship of Apple. A variation on this theme is for the company's board of directors to replace the original CEO with another who has a different leadership style, as Commodore did with Jack Tramiel.

A third strategy is for the entrepreneurial CEO to sell the company when it gets too big to continue with an entrepreneurial style, then set about building a new company. A variation on this theme is merging with another company to bring in new senior managers. This was the strategy of the founder of Conductron, who sold that company to McDonnell Douglas and then went on to found KMS Industries. Similarly, Steven Jobs began to develop a new company after he left Apple.

Finally, a CEO may choose to make the personal and managerial style changes necessary to be able to take the organization to its next growth stage successfully. A critical ingredient in the success of such an attempt is the CEO's willingness to live with less control over the organization and its activities.

The CEO as "Organizational Glue." The CEO who elects to stay with the company and delegate authority to managers now faces another problem. As more than one such person has asked us, "What do I do now? What is my role?" It is likely to be more than a little discomforting for a person who has been hyperactive and involved in virtually all phases of an organization's activities to find that all tangible roles have been delegated and the only thing left is to be a catalyst—a kind of "organizational glue."

The entrepreneurial CEO has been used to being the most versatile person in the orchestra: the individual who could play violin, bass, trombone, drums, or harp. He or she could even be a one-person band. Now, however, the CEO's job is more like that of an orchestra leader. The CEO may not be at all sure that he or she likes or values this new and unfamiliar role. It does not seem to be productive in a concrete way.

In fact, this role is indispensable. Yet the CEO may not be equipped to handle it because of lack of a concept of the role or the skills to perform it or both. Moreover, many CEOs cannot admit weakness by letting anyone guess that they know neither what to do next nor how to do it. Some try to bluff their way through by acting "in an executive manner" and issuing peremptory edicts. Others try to cope by becoming hyperactive, burying themselves in their work. Often, however, this is merely make-work or busy work, an attempt to fool themselves into believing that they are still doing something valuable. A CEO who does not know what to do next but is afraid to admit it and seek for help is setting the stage for future organizational crises.

At this stage of the company's development, the CEO's proper role is to be concerned with the future direction of the enterprise and its long-term objectives. It is to be a strategic leader and a role model for others. Finally, it is to focus on the culture of the enterprise. Each of these aspects of the CEO's new role requires the ability to think abstractly or conceptually about the business rather than merely in terms of concrete products. Unfortunately, many entrepreneurial CEOs either do not have the ability to think conceptually or do not feel comfortable in thinking in this way.

Organizational Issues

In addition to making personal changes, CEOs and other senior managers of entrepreneurial firms must face the challenge of helping their organizations make the transition to professionally managed firms. This section describes some steps they can take to meet that challenge. It recapitulates several themes we have developed throughout this book.

There are four key steps in the process of beginning the transition from an entrepreneurship to a professionally managed organization: (1) conduct an organizational audit, (2) formulate an organizational development plan, (3) implement the plan, and (4) periodically monitor progress. Although the steps are relatively straightforward to explain, in practice they can be quite complex to perform, as illustrated by the case studies in Chapters Four through Six.

Organizational Audit. The first step in planning for the transition from an entrepreneurship to a professionally managed organization is to do an "organizational audit." As you recall from Chapter Two, an organizational audit is a systematic assessment of the strengths, limitations, and developmental needs of an organizational performance: markets, products or services, resources, operational systems, management systems, and corporate culture. The purpose of the audit is to gather data about the organization and its functioning and to use those data to make judgments about the organization's effectiveness and requirements for future development.

Many methods of data collection and analysis may be used in an organizational audit. One effective method is the "focus interview." A focus interview involves meetings between a trained interviewer and selected members of the organization. The interviewer asks a variety of questions dealing with critical aspects of organization performance. The process of the interview and the sequence of the questions is often as important as their content. (Exhibit 2 gives an illustrative sample of types of questions used in an organizational audit.) A number of interviewers may be used, and the information they derive may be pooled in an analysis session.

An organization can do its organizational audit internally. If this is done, an employee trained in organizational development, with a degree from a reputable university and several years of experience, ought to be used. Alternatively, the organization may have an independent consultant perform the audit. Such a person may have a greater degree of objectivity and more experience in conducting such audits than any organization employee.

An organizational audit often includes a special study of the firm's management capabilities and developmental needs. This subaudit may be termed a "Management Development Audit."

Organizational Development Plan. Once the organizational audit has been completed, the next step is to prepare an organizational development plan. As you may recall, this is a plan for the systematic development of an organization in each of the six key areas: markets, products, and so forth. The plan must list the specific objectives and goals that the organization wants to achieve in each key area.

Later Steps. The third step in making the transition is to implement the organizational development plan, and the fourth step is to monitor and revise the plan. Many organizations use an organizational development task force to serve as a planning and advisory group.

Chapters Four through Six described how specific organizations underwent the transitions from one growth stage to the next. As we noted there, organizational development is a lengthy process. It may require time ranging from several months to many years.

Exhibit 2. Sample Questions for Organizational Audit.

1. Market and Market Niche
   1.1 What are the firm's present market segments?
       a. Have the market segments been clearly identified and defined?
       b. Has a strategic market analysis been conducted to answer the following questions:
           (1) Who are our customers?
           (2) What are their needs?
           (3) Through what channels do they buy?
           (4) What is value for them?
       c. What are the key factors that will determine success in satisfying the market's needs?
       d. What is the firm's strategy for competing in its chosen markets?
           (1) Who are the firm's major competitors?
           (2) What are their strengths and limitations?
           (3) What are their comparative advantages?
           (4) What are our comparative advantages?
       e. Is there a good (satisfactory, better than satisfactory, optimal) fit between the market's needs and the firm's strategy?
   1.2 Does the firm have a present or potential market niche (a place where it possesses a comparative advantage)?
       a. If it has a niche, is that niche relatively permanent or perishable?
       b. If it does not have a niche, can one be developed?
2. Products and "Productization"
   2.1 Have the firm's present products been adequately geared (productized) to meet the needs of its present markets?
       a. If not, why?
       b. If so, what can be done to improve the fit?
   2.2 Are there any present or potential market segments for which existing products (ours or competitors') are unsatisfactory?
       a. In what respects?
       b. Can we develop products to capture such markets?
   2.3 How effective is the firm's process (skills) at "productization" (tailoring products to meet market needs)?
3. Resources
   3.1 How adequate are the firm's present resources to implement its strategy?
   3.2 What additional resources are required to implement the firm's market strategy and productization plans?
       a. People
       b. Financial
       c. Facilities
       d. Equipment
       e. Others

During this period it is often useful to repeat che audit process to assess what progress, if any, has been made.

Stages of Growth Beyond Organizational Maturity

Some relatively fortunate organizations will grow to a size in excess of $500 million in annual revenue. This growth will present a set of organizational development problems that is quite different from those encountered during stages I through IV. To assist CEOs in planning for the future of their organizations, this section identifies three stages of growth beyond stage IV: (1) stage V— diversification, (2) stage VI—integration, and (3) stage VII—decline. The key developmental issues encountered in each of these stages are described in the following pages.

Stage V: Diversification. A single product or service line may well take a firm up to between $100 and $500 million in annual revenues. However, it is very unlikely (though not impossible) for a single line of business to enable a firm to grow beyond this point. Thus, if a firm desires to grow further, it will need to replicate the entire cycle of growth stages by developing a new business. Typically, the sheer size of the parent firm will lead it to divisionalize its operations at this point, if it has not already done so. It is likely to develop semiautonomous operating divisions, each focusing on a single line of business.

The upper limit for growth through a single product or line of business may be reached well before a firm generates $500 million in annual revenues. For example, Ashton-Tate, which develops, manufactures, and markets computer software, began facing this problem at about $80 million in revenues. As noted in Chapter Four, Ashton-Tate's main product is a database management software package called dBase II. It seems unlikely that dBASE II, even when combined with its improved version, dBASE III, will be able to carry the firm to a stage of growth beyond its present stage IV. Thus the challenge for Ashton-Tate is to create new products and replicate the growth cycle we have described.

Stage VI: Integration. If an organization is fortunate enough to reach stage VI, it still faces new challenges. At this stage of growth, the enterprise is a "billion-plus" organization. Like Apple

Computer, it may be based on a single line of business, or like Borg-Warner, it may be a family of related businesses.

The key challenge at this stage involves integrating the operations and businesses of the enterprise while maintaining the firm's entrepreneurial spirit. The company has a simultaneous need to have some degree of centralized control over the diverse operating units and to allow divisional managers sufficient freedom to be entrepreneurial in managing their operations. Many companies do not do a good job of striking this delicate balance and lean too much toward organizational control. The price is a loss of entrepreneurial instinct and culture and the creation of institutional bureaucracy that is more concerned with form than with substance.

The problem of integration is, to a great extent, a function of organizational size, complexity, and geographical dispersion. The greater the size of revenues (and, in turn, personnel and transactions), the greater the degree of geographical dispersion, and the greater the degree of business variety, the greater the problems of organizational integration are likely to be.

The problems of organizational integration are made even more complex when two entities merge. The two entities are bound to have different organizational cultures as well as differences in lines of business, and a clash of personalities and power positions is likely to follow in the merger's wake. For example, the merger of Allied Corporation with Signal Corporation is a meeting of billion-dollar behemoths, each with its own corporate culture and operating style. It usually takes years to sort out the differences and integrate the nominally merged entities in a case like this. Similarly, the acquisition of Hughes by General Motors involves an attempt to integrate two very different cultures. GM has a manufacturing, consumer-oriented culture, while Hughes is largely a governmental contractor with a defense-oriented business. Historically, Hughes had been an esoteric community of engineers and scientists rather than of marketing and manufacturing types. The integration of these two diverse entities will require thoughtful leadership.

Stage VII: Decline. Regardless of the initial greatness of a corporation, history shows us that periods of decline are inevitable. In the late nineteenth century, the railroads were the dominant enterprises, but they failed to use their resources to move into other aspects of transportation. In the early part of this century, U.S. Steel was the hallmark of our economy, but it did not retain that position. In the 1950s, General Motors was at its apex, yet it too experienced decline. Other once-great corporations that have experienced organizational decline include National Lead, International Harvester, Chrysler Corporation, Levi Strauss, and Bank of America. For some, decline led the firm to the brink of bankruptcy, while for others it merely led to stunted growth.

The key challenge for a stage VII firm is revitalization. The organization must rebuild itself almost from the ground up. This, in turn, requires that the firm become entrepreneurial in nature once again. Some firms try to achieve revitalization by acquiring other companies that are more entrepreneurial than the purchaser. For example, General Motors has acquired EDS (Electronic Data Systems), founded by entrepreneur H. Ross Perot, as well as Hughes Aircraft in a bid to revitalize. Other organizations that do not yet require revitalization are following a similar strategy. For example, IBM, in a bid to keep its momentum and position itself for the twenty-first century, has acquired Rolm Corporation, the telecommunications company.

We should also note that a firm does not have to reach the multibillion-dollar level before it experiences decline. Decline may occur much sooner. By the time a firm has reached the multibillion-dollar level, however, it is sure to have the seeds of future potential decline within—even though it appears to outsiders to be at the apex of its power.

Some Final Thoughts for the CEO

In this section, I would like to offer some final thoughts to present and potential CEOs of entrepreneurial organizations. These ideas are distilled from my research and consulting work with other CEOs who have gone through the same experience as you, and they may be of use in your own situation.

Understand Your Role. First, it is important to remember that regardless of the number of people working for you, the final responsibility for the development of your organization is not merely yours in the formal sense; it is yours emotionally as well. Your people will look to you as "the Rock." They will expect you to provide support to them, but they will not acknowledge your own needs. There is nothing personal in this. You are simply an object to them. You have all the power, and they perceive you as having the greatest skills. They may even think of you as Superman or Superwoman.

Think Out Loud—Carefully. You will also find that anything you say has enormous impact on the people around you. You may make an offhand comment and find that people have scurried around to do what they thought you sent them a signal to do, even though you were merely thinking out loud. If you do think out loud, you may be viewed as indecisive because people feel that you change your mind too often. Similarly, a hint of a negative comment about one of your employees is likely to echo through the grapevine and reverberate to a much greater extent than you ever intended or believed possible.

Consequently, you may not have anyone to talk to about your own problems in the organization. You may not be able to think out loud. Many CEOs take on confidential advisors for this reason. Doing so is not a sign of weakness or an indication that you can't perform your job; it is simply a functional necessity. You will probably find that you do need to talk things out, and it helps to have someone you trust serving as a sounding board.

Don't Forget the Organizational Plumbing. One of the key tasks in making the successful transition from an entrepreneurial to a professionally managed firm is not to forget the "organizational plumbing," the unglamorous day-to-day systems that are necessary for your organization to operate efficiently and effectively. The organizational plumbing includes the accounting system, the personnel recruitment and training system, credit and collection, advertising, manufacturing, shipping, and operations planning and control. One CEO of a major company going through a rapid growth spurt ignored the company's organizational plumbing and later found that there was a mess in the firm's accounting system that required more than a year to fix. Bank reconciliations had not been done for more than a year, even though the firm's revenues exceeded $300 million.

View Your Organization as a Fine Machine. You should view your company as a machine. It has a variety of parts, and all these parts must be properly connected if the machine is to function. Your managers are key connecting rods in your organizational machine. A major part of their role is to serve as a mechanism of transmission between different parts of the organization.

View Your People as Assets. Your people are a valuable asset. They are just as costly as your furnishings, computers, or other equipment. If you purchase a Mercedes for more than $40,000, you would undoubtedly be willing to spend the necessary $500 to $1500 per year on maintenance. Many of your employees cost you many thousands of dollars. You are more likely to derive a positive return on your investment in them if you provide training and development for your human assets.

Overcome the "Poverty Syndrome." Even if your business did not begin in a garage, you may still be bringing a poverty mentality to the way you operate. One area in which you can no longer afford the "poverty syndrome" is the area of employees and advisors. Hire only the best, and expect to compensate accordingly. Hire fewer people, if necessary, and motivate them to do the work of more. A few highly motivated, well-trained people can often outperform a large number of less qualified people, exerting mere "brute force."

Remember the Omelette. Every chef knows that if you want to make an omelette, you must break some eggs. If you are aware of your firm's growing pains and understand the need for change, you must be prepared to face the negative side of change as well. You will not be able to continue to operate exactly as you have in the past. Both things and people will have to change. Some people will resist change because it is uncomfortable or because change is not in their personal interests. Others will be unable to change. Some people will leave the organization, voluntarily or not. Thus, my final word of advice for CEOs is "Remember the omelette."

Summary

This chapter has examined the personal issues facing the CEO during organizational transitions. It focuses on the changes that the CEO needs to make as his or her organization grows. It also examines the alternatives available to CEOs who face such transitions. The chapter also presents some action steps that may be taken by a CEO whose organization is in transition from one stage of growth to the next. Moreover, the chapter identifies the stages of growth beyond organizational maturity. The chapter also presents some final advice for CEOs of entrepreneurial organizations.

There is no one way to make a successful transition from an entrepreneurship to a professionally managed organization. However, the key to making this change is for the entrepreneur to recognize that the company's former mode of operation will no longer be effective.

All change is accompanied by risk, and many of us feel uncomfortable during the process of change. Unfortunately, the need for organizational transitions and their accompanying personal changes is an inevitability. I hope that this book will assist in making the process of managing such transitions more effective and successful.

Annotated Bibliography:
Key Sources
of Further Information

Part One: A Framework for Developing Successful Organizations

Baty, G. B. *Entrepreneurship for the 80's*. Reston, Va.: Reston, 1981. This book provides a catalogue of concerns for new entrepreneurial ventures. It is not a reference tool for problem solving; rather, it provides a quick overview of potential problems and suggests appropriate information sources.

Carland, J. W., and others. "Differentiating Entrepreneurs from Small Business Owners: A Conceptualization." *Academy of Management Review*, April 1984, pp. 354–359. This review of the literature describes the characteristics of both the entrepreneur and the entrepreneurial venture and proposes two conceptualizations: one for differentiating entrepreneurial ventures from small businesses and another for differentiating entrepreneurs from small business owners/managers. The critical distinctions found between the two involve the entrepreneurs' greater innovative abilities and such entrepreneurial traits as goal orientation, internal locus of control, and the need for independence, responsibility, and power. Risk-taking behavior is rejected as a distinguishing characteristic of entrepreneurship. Definitions of small business venture, entrepreneurial venture, small business owner, and entrepreneur are presented.

Deal, T. D., and Kennedy, A. A. *Corporate Cultures: The Rites and Rituals of Corporate Life.* Reading, Mass.: Addison-Wesley, 1982. In this book the authors suggest that long-term corporate success is dependent on company culture. Specifically, the company's culture must match its strategy. Moreover, a person's success within a company can be a direct result of how well he or she interprets that culture. Through numerous examples the book portrays aspects and types of culture.

Kennedy, A. "Every Employee an Entrepreneur." *Inc.,* April 1984, pp. 108–117. In this interview, Allen Kennedy, coauthor of *Corporate Cultures* (see previous entry), explains his theory in an anthropological perspective, claiming that each company has its own policy and internal behavior that strongly affects its business practice. He predicts a trend away from major corporations and toward entrepreneurship and decentralization. Kennedy discusses his own entrepreneurial venture.

Molz, R. "Entrepreneurial Managers in Large Organizations." *Business Horizons,* September/October 1984, pp. 54–58. This article highlights the importance of entrepreneurial managers in complex, well-established organizations. An entrepreneurial manager can constantly monitor and potentially redefine the organization's objectives as well as meet a changing environment full of new opportunities. How companies can adapt to the entrepreneurial personality is discussed, and strategies for producing innovation within a large company are presented.

Peters, T. J., and Waterman, R. H. *In Search of Excellence: Lessons from America's Best Run Companies.* New York: Harper & Row, 1982. Based on a study of large U.S. corporations, this book outlines eight basic practices that the authors argue are found consistently in excellent organizations. The authors selectively illustrate the occurrence of these practices in a variety of companies.

Powell, J. D., and Bimmerle, C. F. "A Model of Entrepreneurship: Moving Toward Precision and Complexity." *Journal of Small Business Management,* January 1980, pp. 33–36. This article reviews the entrepreneurial process through the use of a model emphasizing the complexity of the venture initiation decision. The model outlines entrepreneurial descriptors, precipitating factors, and venture specific factors, as steps leading to the final entrepreneurial venture. Previous, simplistic models are criticized as having limited predictive utility.

Part Two: Management Strategies for Each Stage of Organizational Growth

Ditlea, S., and Tanjorra, J. "The Birth of an Industry." *Inc.*, January 1982, pp. 64-70. The development of the completely new personal computer software industry is described through examples of the growth of the seven original companies in the field. Case studies of the companies are presented, starting from their inceptions and working through to their current problems, which involve decisions on how to structure their organizations, what products to make, and how to sell those products.

Drucker, P. F. *Innovation and Entrepreneurship: Practice and Principles.* New York: Harper & Row, 1985. Peter Drucker describes a new, dynamic, entrepreneurial economy in America. Through systematic management of organized activity, innovation is no longer left to chance. Drucker examines seven sources for innovative opportunities and explains the practice of entrepreneurship.

Gumpert, D. E., and Stevenson, H. E. "The Heart of Entrepreneurship." *Harvard Business Review*, March/April 1985, pp. 85-94. The steps of the entrepreneurial process are outlined, along with the necessary structure and characteristics a firm should have to maintain an entrepreneurial environment. The administrative state of mind, whose focus involves guarding resources and reducing risk, is contrasted with that of the entrepreneur.

Hoy, F., and Vaught, B. C. "The Rural Entrepreneur: A Study in Frustration." *Journal of Small Business Management*, January 1980, pp. 18-24. This study of 150 rural Texas entrepreneurs lists the major problems faced by these businesses and shows that there are certain types of problems—such as personnel problems, government regulations, and economic conditions—that because of their external nature frustrate managerial attempts to overcome them. Entrepreneurs cite these issues as major problems inhibiting the successful operation of their businesses, yet they do not seek outside help. They do seek outside help for what they perceive as the most significant types of problems over which they feel they have control, such as marketing-related problems. The study concludes that more education is needed in the area of goal expectancy. Goal accomplishment, as opposed to the skills training, should be emphasized so that frustration will be minimized as awareness of control is gained by management.

Kidder, T. *The Soul of a New Machine.* New York: Avon, 1981. This narrative explores the development of a new computer at Data General Corporation. It illustrates the dynamics of new product development within an entrepreneurial organization.

"Prophets of the New Age." *Inc.,* April 1984, pp. 81–91. Case studies are presented that depict the beginnings and subsequent successes of six entrepreneurs who have formed highly profitable corporations. Included among the six are Steven Jobs of Apple Computer and Fred Smith of Federal Express.

Richman, T. "Going Their Way." *Inc.,* December 1983, pp. 70–76. This article reviews the achievements of America's fastest growing private companies, named in the "Inc. 500." Brief case studies of the top twenty-five entrepreneurial companies are presented, and characteristics shared by all the companies are described.

Part Three: Mastering the Tools of Professional Management

Strategic Planning

Brandt, S. C. *Strategic Planning in Emerging Companies.* Reading, Mass.: Addison-Wesley, 1981. This book provides the basic perspective necessary for strategic planning and outlines its various dimensions. The author integrates comments on organizational units and corporate culture within the framework of strategic planning.

Glueck, W. F., and Jauch, L. R. *Strategic Management and Business Policy.* New York: McGraw-Hill, 1984. This text walks the reader through the strategic management process, emphasizing the need for continuous planning. Focus is on the environment and internal competitive advantages. Choices and evaluation of strategy provide a firm understanding of the model.

Lorange, P. *Implementation of Strategic Planning.* Englewood Cliffs, N.J.: Prentice-Hall, 1982. Lorange provides an overview of the issues involved in implementing strategic plans. In addition, a considerable amount of discussion relating to planning systems provides a framework to evaluate a strategic planning system.

Steiner, G. A. *Top Management Planning.* New York: Macmillan, 1969. Steiner offers readers an important foundation in and overview of corporate planning terminology and concepts. A top management perspective places the emphasis on overall results for the business while also discussing planning in many of the functional areas.

Control Systems

Koenig, J., Flamholtz, D. T., and Flamholtz, E. G. *Organizational Control Systems.* New York: Touche Ross & Co., 1985. A monograph that outlines control and control systems, this book also addresses the role of accounting in organizational control. It considers the organization's need for control and how to evaluate this need.

Kotter, J. P., Schlesinger, L. A., and Sathe, V. *Organization.* Homewood, Ill.: Irwin, 1979. Texts, cases, and readings on the management of organizational design and change attempt to bridge the gap between social science research and practical management concerns. The authors emphasize that through design and control, organizational effort can be coordinated to accomplish objectives. Further, they discuss how to implement changes in control systems.

Newman, W. H. *Constructive Control.* Englewood Cliffs, N.J.: Prentice-Hall, 1975. This book describes how managerial control can obtain positive responses through ties to desired results. The structural and behavioral elements of control are explored along with their applications in a variety of operations. Finally, systems to coordinate controls are reviewed.

Management Development

Cox, C., and Beck, J. *Management Development*. New York: Wiley, 1984. Through a selection of articles, the book deals with many current issues of management development. Issues treated include women in management, managerial obsolescence, and responsibility for training.

London, M. *Developing Managers*. San Francisco: Jossey-Bass, 1985. Throughout this study of career motivation, guidelines and issues are brought to the attention of management. In addition, it reviews types of training programs and their potentials and includes a description of strategies for coping with mid-career crises.

Lopez, F. E., Rockmore, B. W., and Kesselman, G. A. "The Development of an Integrated Career Planning Program at Gulf Power Company," in H. G. Heneman and D. T. Schwab (eds.), *Perspectives on Personnel/Human Resource Management* (Homewood, Ill.: Irwin, 1982). This article provides a model and case study for developing a career matrix for management development.

Leadership

Likert, R. *The Human Organization*. New York: McGraw-Hill, 1967. A classic, this book deals with leadership styles and their effects on the management and value of human resources. Likert postulates four different styles or systems of management, which parallel the first four styles of management described in Chapter Ten of the present book.

Maccoby, M. *The Leader*. New York: Simon & Schuster, 1981. Maccoby challenges the traditional concepts of management and proposes a picture of the leaders who will come to dominate in the United States. Through descriptions of six types of leaders, both in business and government, the author documents leadership principles and then goes further to discuss the development of leadership.

Part Four: Role of the Entrepreneur in a Growing and Changing Company

Burgelman, R. A. "A Process Model of Internal Corporate Venturing in the Diversified Major Firm." *Administrative Science Quarterly*, June 1983, pp. 223–244. The focus of this field study is the process through which a diversified major firm transforms R&D activities into a new business through internal corporate venturing (ICV). The relationship between project development and business development is specifically examined, as well as how new organizational units developed around new businesses become integrated into the operating system of the corporation. The components necessary for a successful ICV effort are presented.

Grove, A. S. *High Output Management*. New York: Random House, 1983. The president of Intel who is one of its founders describes his concept of Intel's management philosophy. The book stresses an output-orientation and introduces the concept of management leverage to team management. Finally, an analogy to sports is drawn to illustrate obtaining peak individual performances among the business team.

Levinson, H., and Rosenthal, S. *CEO*. New York: Basic Books, 1984. This book outlines the practice of leadership by CEOs. Through documented interviews at six well-known companies, the authors provide a glimpse of what leadership involves in a highly organized setting.

Steiner, G. A. *The New CEO*. New York: Macmillan, 1983. This book reviews the changing social and political environment of U.S. business and the extent to which the forces that shape it compel the CEOs of large firms to involve themselves in external affairs. These new responsibilities, particularly in the public policy area, require CEOs to have a variety of talents and the ability to balance constituent interests.

Index

227